REBECCA J BERRY

Possible

25 READINGS TO RECOVER THE WONDER OF CHRISTMAS

Printed in the United States of America

First Printing, 2023

ISBN 978-1-7326926-3-3

Unless otherwise noted, Scripture quotations are from THE HOLY BIBLE, NEW INTERNATIONAL VERSION®, NIV® Copyright © 1973, 1978, 1984, 2011 by Biblica, Inc.® Used by permission. All rights reserved worldwide.
Scripture quotations noted as NASB® are from the New American Standard Bible®, Copyright © 1960, 1971, 1977, 1995, 2020 by The Lockman Foundation. Used by permission. All rights reserved. lockman.org
Scripture quotations noted as TLV are from Tree of Life (TLV) Translation of the Bible. Copyright © 2015 by The Messianic Jewish Family Bible Society.
Scripture quotations noted as KJV are from the King James Version which is in the public domain.

Rebecca J. Berry, publisher
Plotting Possibility

For my uncle,
Dr. Gary L. Buterbaugh,
who believed in me more than I knew,
and who loved Jesus with his whole heart.

Contents

Author's Note

Merry Christmas!

I am so excited you're joining me this Christmas season. If you're feeling the stress of the season and your tinsel is in a tangle, then you can rest assured that I get it. Boy, do I get it. And it's my prayer that God meets you just where you are this Christmas. That your heart will be quickened with new wonder like fresh snow falling to beautify the barren, weary earth.

This book has twenty-five readings. If you prefer, you can read one each day starting on December 1st, and you'll finish this book on Christmas Day. If you're like me and daily readings somehow become impossible, fear not! The last readings are about the Magi and traditionally their visit is celebrated on Epiphany on January 6th. This gives you two extra weeks to get all the readings in. Quite honestly though, it doesn't make any difference to me or anyone else when you read this book. Finish it on Valentine's Day, or grab it for a read by the pool next summer. There's just one rule with the books I write–that you seek Jesus on every page.

This devotional is a little different. I've written seven monologues from the point of view of someone in the Christmas story. All of the monologues are heavily grounded in scripture (anything word-for-word from scripture is **bold**). I first heard the phrase 'sanctified imagination' several years back, and that's how I describe my creative work. My imagination is at play, but it is soaked in scripture and bathed in prayer. I encourage you to activate your imagination as you read. St. Ignatius believed that by using our imaginative powers to immerse us into gospel narratives, we can "enter God's Word and hear the Word as spoken personally to us today."[1]

---

[1] Timothy M. Gallagher.

Between the monologues are expository readings. I provide scripture passages to read, a deep dive into the meaning and context, and then a few reflection questions for you to ponder. I have a two-pronged approach to this book: 1) that nothing is impossible with God, and 2) no word from God will ever fail. As we read the nativity story with fresh eyes, we will see these truths in living color.

As you go, you will notice some repetition of ideas, imagery, and key insights. Think of how a weaver creates a beautiful tapestry, thread by thread, back and forth across the loom until it is complete. This is how God has woven his story. These are threads only he could weave through time and space. As I've written this book, God has drawn my eyes to some of these narrative threads, and I pray it fills you with awe as it has me.

Okay, I think that'll wrap up this little note from me to you. Before we get started, I'm going to pray for us.

Dear Lord Jesus, we're about to get wrapped up in the story of you coming to rescue us. Renew our curiosity and wonder for this story. Come, join us here and change us for good. We ask these things in your precious and powerful name—Amen.

Ready? Let's go. The best gift this season may be what you find tucked in the glorious good news of the gospel.

In His Love,

1) Prologue

"For nothing will be impossible with God." – Luke 1:37 (NASB)

When I was small anything seemed possible, especially at Christmas time. My lists for Santa, I must confess, were quite lengthy and fantastic. A baby reindeer. Rainbow colored puppies. My own TV. And VCR.

Year after year, I dreamed of the possibilities. Undaunted by the fact that I never woke up to a baby reindeer under the Christmas tree. I don't know when exactly I outgrew Santa. It wasn't a traumatizing event. I suppose I just understood at some point that it was my parents and not a jolly old elf. And that certainly explained why I never got that reindeer.

In my freshman year of college, I had an evening class. I loved walking back to the dorm on brisk winter evenings. Bundled up against the wind, I'd gaze up at the sky. If it was overcast it was like a blanket thrown over my little corner of the world, and if it was clear then my star-friends were there to wink at me the whole way home. I remember thinking maybe I loved winter best because I was born in December and there was just so much magic in it.

But sometimes now the Christmas magic feels a little thin. The movies tell us it's the skepticism of our age. Maybe that explains why Santa is having a rough go of it. Fox News says there's a war on Christmas. Personally, I think that's nonsense.

I think we're responsible. Us. You and me and our busyness and distractions and to-do lists and traditions and festivities. I bet your December is packed tight, isn't it? Is your heart rate climbing a little right now as you think about all the gifts to buy and people to see and commitments on your calendar?

No wonder we've lost our sense of wonder. Who has time to gaze up at an endless sky on a cold winter's night and wink at the stars? Who has time to slowly ponder through the Advent season, marveling at the miracle of God dwelling among us? There's too much to do. So many other responsibilities elbow worship and wonder out of the way. Then, we show up at the Christmas Eve service hoping it fills our cup. And hopefully, it does a little. I, for one, get all teary at a candlelight service and fellowship of my church family. But I think there's so much more for us—more true wonder, more true worship, more true joy.

How do we reclaim the glittering possibilities of the season? Netflix has some great Santa movies... but that's not really the point, is it? That's not the magic we need. It won't fill our souls.

No, if we want our wonder back it has to start with worship. And if we want to worship, we have to start with Jesus.

His story is so familiar to us. Like a favorite old quilt, passed down through generations. We pull it out of storage every year to wrap around us, to rest in its softness and familiarity.

Oh, it can be such a treasure to know Scripture so well that it feels like that soft family quilt—like home. Yet sometimes we need to shake out the wrinkles and look at it with fresh eyes. To marvel at the colors and textures and artistry.

Close your eyes and picture this quilt. Imagine that each piece is one part of the story. This square was sewn with care by Elizabeth's wrinkled hands, and this one by Mary's nimble fingers; this patch is lacy with threads of angel wings, and this one is thick with warm lamb's wool. It's a breathtaking masterpiece! Don't you just ache to hear the stories behind these patches?

Keep reading.

In the pages that follow are narratives from various members of the Christmas story. Imagine they've come over to your home on a frosty winter evening to share a mug of something hot and tell you their story. As you lean in, you catch a glimpse of the sky and a star throws you a wink. Already the wonder is rekindling.

"For no word from God will ever fail."-- Luke 1:37 (NIV)

God, I ask you to open my mind and my heart to you. Show me your faithfulness, reveal the thread of your plan, and the artistry of your Word. I'm ready for wonder. –Amen

- Do you still feel wonder at Christmas? Where do you find little glimmers of Christmas magic? What are your favorite traditions?
- Does the story of Jesus's birth fill you with wonder? Why or why not?

2) The Word Dwelled Among Us

"The light shines in the darkness,
and the darkness has not overcome it." – John 1:5

★ **Read John 1: 1-18**

I absolutely love the Gospel of John. I've always had a sniggling feeling that we're not supposed to have favorite books of the Bible because '*all* scripture is God-breathed and useful for teaching' (2 Tim 3:16, emphasis mine). However, I can't help it. I absolutely do play favorites when it comes to the writings of John. He's my fave. We're something of kindred spirits, I think. When you read through his writings you can't help but notice the recurring metaphor of dark and light. It beats like a resounding drum. 'God is light, and in him there is no darkness at all.' (1 John 1:5). And I am one who has been desperate for the light.

Depression is one of my greatest enemies. Every time I read John's words– 'the light shines in the darkness, and the darkness has *not* overcome it' (emphasis mine)-- I'm infused with a good dose of hope again. The darkness cannot overcome the light. In those dark nights of the soul that comes to us all, Jesus shines. We're never alone in the dark.

To be clear, I'm not suggesting that John also struggled with depression or mental health. But he did have a fascination with light. He must have known darkness. We know he had a temper. Jesus didn't nickname him and his brother the 'Sons of Thunder' for nothing. (Mark 3:17).

And he lived in spiritually dark times. The first century was a noisy place with sectarian feuds, hypocrisy, religiosity, and hedonism. Into this darkness, Jesus came. And John watched him up close and in person. He saw how the Light of Mankind changed mankind with love.

The other pervasive theme in John's writings is that of love. He's been nicknamed the 'Apostle of Love'. The Son of Thunder became the Apostle of Love. That's no small thing. Let's not gloss over it. A young guy with temper issues became a champion for love. John didn't achieve this on his own by trying really hard to be a good person. He didn't check out a bunch of books on anger management from the library, or sign up for a webinar. He knew Jesus. He walked with Jesus. And Jesus left his indelible mark of love on John's very soul.

When we read John's words, we find out that's why Jesus came here. One of the most famous Bible verses was penned by John. I'll share it in the KJV because that's how I memorized it as a very little girl: 'For God so loved the world that he gave his only begotten son that whosoever believeth in him should not perish but have everlasting life.' (John 3:16)

Love, my friends. It's a beautiful thing. Love and light. That's what John tells us about Jesus.

I'll never get over the beauty of these opening words of John's Gospel. Jesus is the Word. He was there in the beginning. Creation happened through him–the Word–as God spoke the entire universe into being. Every teeny plankton and ginormous black hole exists because of Jesus. There's power here. Majesty. Glory. It's incredible.

Then John tells us that the Word became flesh and dwelled among us. He took off his royal robes and settled for baby diapers. Jesus arrived here a helpless baby who needed to be fed, burped, and changed just like every other baby on planet Earth. He grew up 'in wisdom and stature, and in favor with God and man', yes–but also as a refugee and as a poor kid from a small town. (Matt 2:41) He sweat when he was hot. Wept when he was heartbroken. And laughed when he was happy. Just like the rest of us.

We read in John that when Jesus came the world didn't recognize him. The very people he came to save rejected him. That's heartbreaking, isn't it? Jesus experienced rejection time and again.

> "The God who created matter took shape within it, as an artist might become a spot on a painting or a playwright a character within his own play. God wrote a story, only using real characters, on the pages of real history. The Word became flesh."--Philip Yancey

Most often from the people who should've been the first to recognize him. As we go forward, we're going to read many of the Old Testament prophecies regarding the Messiah. Yet it was the most learned who missed Jesus. Heaven forbid it be the same for us. I don't want us to miss him because we're expecting something else. Or, perhaps more poignantly for us, because we think we already know his story. My friends, there is always more that Jesus wants to reveal to us about himself. Let's not reject his invitation to know him more.

Those who did believe in Jesus received an incredible gift. A gift that far surpasses anything you could put under your Christmas tree. He gave them the right to become children of God. His brothers and sisters. Family the likes of which we have never experienced. There's a danger that we've started taking this for granted. We recite it like kids at school.

Because of sin, we are strangers to God. Or worse, in our rebellion we act as enemies towards God. In God's perfect plan, enemies cannot be family. We can't truly know him until the debt of our rebellion has been paid, and we've come under his lordship. The trouble is, we can't do this on our own. The only acceptable payment for sin is death. If I die, then that's it—I died in my sin. I have no hope. There's only darkness here.

This is why it matters so much that Jesus is the light, and that he came and dwelled among us. 'He is the atoning sacrifice for our sins, and not only for ours but also for the sins of the whole world'. (1 John 2:2). Jesus came so we would no longer be strangers. He paid the penalty for our rebellion. He made it so he can be our Lord, and lead us in pathways that honor God. Although he didn't break it, he fixed what was broken.

'The Word became flesh and made his dwelling among us. We have seen his glory, the glory of the one and only Son, who came from the Father, full of grace and truth.'-- John 1:14

Dear Lord, I pray that when I reach the end of this book I'll be able to join John in saying that I have seen the glory of Jesus, of the one and only son, who came from the Father, full of grace and truth. I can think of no better Christmas gift I could possibly ask for. —Amen.

- Close your eyes and imagine how you want to feel this Christmas. Write down some of the words that float to the surface. Pray over those words and ask Jesus to show you his will for you this season.

3) Elizabeth's Story

"In those days John the Baptist came, preaching in the wilderness of Judea
and saying, "Repent, for the kingdom of heaven has come near."
This is he who was spoken of through the prophet Isaiah:
"A voice of one calling in the wilderness, 'Prepare the way for the Lord,
make straight paths for him.'"–Matthew 3:1-3

You want to know about my boy John? The one they call 'The
Baptizer'. Yes, I can tell you about John. My beautiful, wild boy. My
miracle. Let's see, well, I suppose it all started with prayer.

For years we prayed for a son. We promised we would dedicate him to the
Lord. That we would raise him to be a good Jewish man, a priest like his
father. But no child came. Month after month. Year after year. My friends
all had babies. My relatives all had babies. But no baby ever filled my womb
with kicks and hiccups. It was the greatest disappointment of my life.

It was the shame of my life too. After all, for my people, it's a woman's great
glory to be a mother. People assume if you aren't blessed with a child, then
you must be cursed–and you're only cursed because of some sin against
God.

And my husband is a priest! So there was no hiding our shame. The entire
community was well aware of Zechariah and his barren wife. Barren. That's
me. Empty, dry, useless. My husband could have divorced me once he
realized I was barren, but Zechariah is such a good man. He would never
add to my shame in that way. Never. No, we endured this sadness together.

Eventually, I suppose, we gave up hope. Or at least trying. After a certain age, it seemed ridiculous to believe God would answer our prayers differently. I tried to content myself with loving the children around me and stayed busy keeping a tidy Jewish home. Our days were quiet, but we had gotten used to that. There was something safe in the routine we created. Mundane, perhaps, but predictable. Comfortable even in our heartache.

Then, the time came around for Zechariah's division to be on duty at the temple. The priests are organized into twenty-four divisions and Zechariah belongs to the division of Abijah–eighth on the list. Although, there are so many priests now that each family can only serve twice a year, and just for one week at a time. I remember before he left he was hoping the lots would fall to him to offer the incense on the altar. It's a once-in-a-lifetime honor, you know. Although Zechariah was getting on in his years, the lots had yet to fall in his favor. Looking back, I can see how God had planned it all and the timing was just right. But the years of longing and waiting had taken their toll on my husband.

I remained at home. He would only be gone a week, and he'd be busy serving in the temple. So, I stayed, hoping and praying Zechariah's moment would finally come. Well, the lots fell and Zechariah was chosen to burn the incense on the altar and offer prayers to God for all our people. Of course, I had no idea that my husband had encountered an angel when he performed his duty at the temple. Not until he returned at the end of his week of service....and he couldn't speak!

Now, ladies, if we're honest we all have moments when we wish our men would lose their ability to speak, but let me tell you, when it happens, well, it's terrifying. Zechariah left for the temple at the beginning of the week perfectly fine and normal, he came home completely mute. In writing, he explained he was chosen to burn the incense and offer prayers. Just as he was preparing the incense an angel appeared. Gabriel. And Gabriel gave him the most incredible news:

"Do not be afraid, Zechariah; your prayer has been heard. Your wife Elizabeth will bear you a son, and you are to call him John. He will be a joy and delight to you, and many will rejoice because of his birth, for he will be great in the sight of the Lord. He is never to take wine or other fermented drink, and he will be filled with the Holy Spirit even before he is born. He will bring back many of the people of Israel to the Lord their God. And he will go on before the Lord, in the spirit and power of Elijah, to turn the hearts of the parents to their children and the disobedient to the wisdom of the righteous—to make ready a people prepared for the Lord."

Well, to be honest, I'm not sure what I would've said to an angel of the Most High God at that moment, but unfortunately, Zechariah questioned him. He said, **"How can I be sure of this? I am an old man and my wife is well along in years."**

Apparently, the angel did not like to be questioned. He told my husband, **"I am Gabriel. I stand in the presence of God, and I have been sent to speak to you and to tell you this good news. And now you will be silent and not able to speak until the day this happens, because you did not believe my words, which will come true at their appointed time."**

Now here I was with a mute husband and this divine revelation that I would have a baby. Not just any baby either but one who would have the spirit and power of Elijah. The one who would prepare the way for the

Lord. The Messiah. The one we'd been praying to come to us for hundreds of years. I think you'll understand when I tell you I needed to sit down.

Sure enough, in due time, I conceived a child. Oh, I could scarcely believe it even though I know the word of God is always true. Just when I thought we'd had our generous share of miracles, my darling cousin came to visit. I was in my sixth month then. When Mary came into our home and greeted me, my baby boy leaped in my womb! This barren belly which had never felt a fluttering or a kick or a hiccup. My son leaped for joy when he heard her voice.

And I was filled with the Holy Spirit. Me! The one who was barren and empty was filled with the Holy Spirit and so was this bouncing baby in my womb. Never in my life had I dreamed of such a wondrous thing. I couldn't help but cry out:

"Blessed are you among women, and blessed is the child you will bear! But why am I so favored, that the mother of my Lord should come to me? As soon as the sound of your greeting reached my ears, the baby in my womb leaped for joy. Blessed is she who has believed that the Lord would fulfill his promises to her!"

Mary and I praised the Lord with all our hearts that day. Our hearts were full of joy and wonder that both of us should be carrying sons– impossible, but possible with God. You know, there are some days you remember all your life. In my old age and all my years, I can tell you that was one of the best.

When the time came, my son was born. Our relatives and neighbors all wanted to call him Zechariah, after his father. But we insisted on John, just as Gabriel had told us. When Zechariah wrote that down for all to see, his voice returned. He'd had quite some time to think of what he'd say when this moment came.

Let me tell you, his song of praise was beautiful. Zechariah recalled God's covenant with his people–his promise to send us a Messiah who would rescue us. And the blessing he spoke over our son was a confirmation of the message the angel had delivered to him. All doubt was gone. My husband's well of faith overflowed as he declared, **"And you, my child, will be called a prophet of the Most High; for you will go on before the Lord to prepare the way for him, to give his people the knowledge of salvation through the forgiveness of their sins, because of the tender mercy of our God by which the rising sun will come to us from heaven to shine on those living in darkness and in the shadow of death, to guide our feet into the path of peace."**

I'd never been so happy to hear him praise God. Or to be one of God's chosen people. I never imagined I would be one God would actually choose to serve in such a way. To be the mother of the Voice in the Wilderness. Oh, every time I think of it I get chills– even the hair on my arms just stands up to praise God!

We raised our son just as God had instructed. We made sure that he never had any wine or fruits of the vine, and we never cut his hair. More than just rules, we raised John to be who God created him to be. There were plenty of folks who didn't understand us or him. People expected us to raise John to be like his father. A priest in the line of Aaron! But we raised John to be just exactly who God created him to be, who he called him to be.

And so my baby boy had a wild streak. One I never did quite tame. I felt he would need it to serve God with all his body, heart, and soul.

John lives in the wilderness now. He wears clothes made of camel hair and eats locusts and wild honey. They call him 'The Baptizer' because he preaches repentance and baptizes those who turn back to God in the Jordan River. He's doing exactly what God said he would do. Standing next to his father, they couldn't be any more different. But Zechariah and I are proud of our son. He truly has been our joy and delight. Our wild boy.[2]

- Have you ever been shocked by an answer to prayer? How did you respond when the answer came?
- Elizabeth was unfairly judged by her community when they assumed her barrenness was because of sin. Yet she was seen, loved, and chosen by God. How can we hold onto the truth God offers when we feel misunderstood by others?

---

[2] A Note from Rebecca: Because Zechariah and Elizabeth were advanced in years when John was conceived, I'm not positive they lived to see him become known as The Baptizer. However, we don't know for certain. For the purpose of this study, I felt it was okay to imagine Elizabeth and Zechariah living long enough to see their boy all grown up and living out his calling. It doesn't change how we read, interpret, and apply the scriptures concerning this amazing, little family. One thing for sure, they *knew* it would happen just as they had been told because God had promised and they had been faithful.

4) Voice in the Wilderness

"And you, my child, will be called a prophet of the Most High;
for you will go on before the Lord to prepare the way for him..."
-- Luke 1: 76

★**Read Luke 1: 5-23, 57-80**

Here we are on the cusp of the season with Thanksgiving fresh in our minds and CHRISTMAS thundering down the mountain in a glittery avalanche of expectations and tissue paper. I crack open my Bible to get centered, and what do I find in the first chapter of Luke? This story about a childless old couple. A priest with prayers so old and thin that they don't hold much faith anymore. I'll be painstakingly honest with you—sometimes my faith looks like Zechariah's. How about you?

Let's really lean in here and look at what Gabriel revealed to Zechariah. Maybe we'll be able to give him some grace (even if Gabriel didn't!). The words start out really good, right? Wouldn't you love it if an angel appeared and assured you that God had heard your prayers? That you're going to get the very thing you've for which you've been praying? Gabriel goes so far as to tell Zechariah that his son will be a joy and delight, and that many will rejoice at his birth. Wow! What an assurance!

Next comes a directive. Gabriel tells Zechariah that his son is never to drink wine or other fermented drinks. This is part of the Nazirite vow which is explained in Numbers 6. Those who take a Nazarite vow are consecrated to the Lord. They cannot drink alcohol, they cannot eat anything produced from the vine (grapes or raisins), they cannot cut their hair, and they cannot have any contact with a dead body—even a family member. At first blush, perhaps these rules seem more odd than anything. For us, it may not be that hard to follow. However, in the ancient world, wine was a common drink. The fruits of the vine were a regular staple of their diet. They were not clinically removed from death as we are with hospitals and funeral homes. To be forbidden to have any contact at all with a dead body, even your parents, was a significant thing. Of all the rules here, maybe the one about haircuts seems easiest to follow. Although, imagine the heat of all that hair on the back of your neck in the desert.

Gabriel goes on to say that the child will be filled with the Holy Spirit even before he is born. Being filled with the Holy Spirit worked differently for those before Christ than it does for those of us living after his resurrection and ascension. When we look at the Old Testament (and that would, in a way, include this moment in time here with Zechariah) we see that the Holy Spirit did not often dwell within people. Typically, the Spirit would come upon someone and allow them to prophesy, and then depart. This promise regarding John is quite different. Unlike anyone else before or since, John was filled with the Spirit from conception.

Maybe this is where Gabriel started to lose Zechariah. Joy and delight? Yes, sign me up. Nazarite vows? Sounds hard, but okay. Filled with the Holy Spirit from birth? Um...alright. Then, in verse 16, Gabriel reveals that John will bring people back to the Lord. That sounds good, especially for the son of a priest. But let's not gloss over the next verse. In 17, it is said that John will go in the spirit and power of Elijah.

Okay–this is huge. This may be the part that made Zechariah shake his head. For first-century Jews, Elijah was *the* prophet. He was up there with Moses in greatness. The stories of Elijah's ministry had been handed down for generations. And they knew that it was foretold that Elijah would be sent to them. In fact, this prophecy was so important to the Jews that they set an empty place for him at Passover.

Let's take a minute to talk about this. In 2 Kings 2, Elijah is swept into heaven in a chariot of fire. Honestly, if you've studied the life of Elijah, this bizarre story seems to fit. He was an incredible prophet who defied evil King Ahab and Queen Jezebel. The miracles he was able to perform through the power of the Holy Spirit are some of my favorites (personal aside: if we'd had a second son, his name would have been Elijah). The important takeaway today is that Elijah ascended into heaven and did not experience physical death.

Turn in your Bible to **Malachi 4:5-6.** What do you notice about Malachi and its position in the Bible? What about these verses specifically?

These were the last words recorded before the 'intertestamental period'. That's a lofty way of saying that four hundred years of silence followed. That single page you have in your Bible that separates the OT from the NT represents four centuries. Centuries of struggle and conquest, suffering and *silence*. God answered prayers and took care of his people because he remained true to his promises, but there were no prophets. No voice speaking to them. For generations, Jews held onto their history and their hope for a future. A hope revealed to them by prophets, followed by four hundred long years of silence.

Until now. Until this moment in the temple between a priest and an angel. When Gabriel said, "And he will go on before the Lord, in the spirit and power of Elijah, to turn the hearts of the fathers to their children and the disobedient to the wisdom of the righteous—to make ready a people prepared for the Lord." (Luke 1:17 NIV) This may be more than

Zechariah can believe.

Four hundred years of silence were just shattered like a rock hitting glass. The sound here is shocking. It's perhaps one thing to be told that God has heard your prayers and you're being blessed with a child. It seems like another thing entirely to be told that this child is the long-awaited 'Elijah'. The one that would prepare the way for the Lord. Put yourself in Zechariah's shoes and ponder what he's just been told.

I don't know about you, but I would probably need to sit down and just take that in. Maybe that's what Zechariah should have done. Instead, it seems that he blurted out the first thing that popped into his head. "How can I be sure of this? I am an old man and my wife is well along in years." (Luke 1: 18)

Dumbfounded by the incredible revelation of the angel, Zechariah struggled to believe it was really true. After a lifetime of prayers and disappointment, he couldn't believe it was truly possible. Yeah, I'm in no place to sit in judgment of Zechariah. I get it.

Gabriel, however, seems righteously offended. Indignant. Annoyed. Imagine his tone and stature as he declared, "I am Gabriel. I stand in the presence of God, and I have been sent to speak to you and to tell you this good news." (Luke 1:19)

You can almost see Zechariah shrug his shoulders helpless and confused and unsure, and then Gabriel pulls himself to his full majestic height. For some reason, I imagine a hand drifting to a scabbard at his side. This is an angelic being full of power. And complete confidence. He doesn't double-check his smartphone to make sure he got the assignment right. He doesn't put a finger to an earpiece and make sure he's hearing things correctly from some heavenly dispatcher. No, he's *sure*. He is certain.

Poor Zechariah goes from dumbfounded to truly dumb– "temporarily unable or unwilling to speak" (Google definition). However, God's plans do not change. Zechariah's weak faith does not impede the plan God intends to set in motion. No, this plan has been in the works for centuries, millennia, perhaps prior to the first sands of time as we know it ever being poured. Zechariah is not going to get in the way of that. There's a consequence for his lack of faith–he wants a sign, Gabriel gave him a sign! But it does not change the prophecy or its fulfillment.

Now let's fast-forward to the birth of John. In first-century Palestine, when a baby was born all the neighbors, relatives, and friends would come to the house. They brought instruments and food in preparation for a big celebration. If the baby was a boy, the celebration would begin. If the baby was a girl, they would leave in quiet disappointment.

So, here we see all the neighbors and relatives rejoiced. Elizabeth has brought forth a son! And all these folks assumed the baby will be named after his father. When Elizabeth said that the child is to be named John, they argued with her and asked Zechariah for confirmation.

When he wrote that his son was named John, the curse was removed! Zechariah declard that his son's name *is* John. His name was already given to him by God. The name 'John' is derived from the Hebrew word Yohanan (or Johanan). It means 'God is gracious' or 'graced by God'.

Zechariah moved from unbelief to belief. No longer dubious, he was sure that the message he was given was true. I don't think it's only because he's now holding this child of promise in his arms. No, I think Zechariah's months of silence formed his faith. Perhaps we also need to be still and quiet before the Lord, and let our faith be shaped.

The Holy Spirit is on the move in Zechariah's family! First his (unborn) son, then his wife, and now Zechariah himself is filled with the Spirit. Oftentimes, first-century Jews often prayed standing up with their hands lifted high. This is exactly how I imagine Zechariah at this moment. He is bold. He is confident. No longer that frail, unsure old man. He believes that the Word of God never fails. The words Zechariah spoke here are powerful and beautiful.

The history Zechariah repeated is one we see repeated again and again throughout the Old Testament. Only now, Zechariah is speaking in the present tense. God *has come*. He's here with us.

Then, Zechariah's prophecy turned toward his son. He shifted from the macro vision of God's plan of redemption for all people to the micro vision of God's plan for his son. This is the moment where we see that Zechariah truly had full confidence in Gabriel's message.

Let's look at John all grown up for just a moment to see how well this prophecy held up. After all, one of our thesis statements is that 'no word from God will ever fail'.

In Matthew 3:4 we read: 'John's clothes were made of camel's hair, and he had a leather belt around his waist. His food was locusts and wild honey.' If we turn back in the Old Testament to 2 Kings 1:8 we read this: 'They replied, "He had a garment of hair and had a leather belt around his waist." The king said, "That was Elijah the Tishbite."'

It's uncanny, isn't it? Let's check out two more passages very quickly.

Now this was John's testimony when the Jewish leaders in Jerusalem sent priests and Levites to ask him who he was. He did not fail to confess, but confessed freely, "I am not the Messiah." They asked him, "Then who are you? Are you Elijah?"
He said, "I am not."
"Are you the Prophet?"
He answered, "No."
Finally they said, "Who are you? Give us an answer to take back to those who sent us. What do you say about yourself?"
John replied in the words of Isaiah the prophet, "I am the voice of one calling in the wilderness, 'Make straight the way for the Lord.'"
Now the Pharisees who had been sent questioned him, "Why then do you baptize if you are not the Messiah, nor Elijah, nor the Prophet?"
"I baptize with water," John replied, "but among you stands one you do not know. He is the one who comes after me, the straps of whose sandals I am not worthy to untie."-- John 1:19-27

'As John's disciples were leaving, Jesus began to speak to the crowd about John: "What did you go out into the wilderness to see? A reed swayed by the wind? If not, what did you go out to see? A man dressed in fine clothes? No, those who wear fine clothes are in kings' palaces.Then what did you go out to see? A prophet? Yes, I tell you, and more than a prophet. This is the one about whom it is written: 'I will send my messenger ahead of you, who will prepare your way before you.' Truly I tell you, among those born of women there has not risen anyone greater than John the Baptist; yet whoever is least in the kingdom of heaven is greater than he. From the days of John the Baptist until now, the kingdom of heaven has been subjected to violence, and violent people have been raiding it. For all the Prophets and the Law prophesied until John. And if you are willing to accept it, he is the Elijah who was to come. Whoever has ears, let them hear.'-- Matthew 11:7-15

There's no question that John's contemporaries noticed he was 'in the spirit and power of Elijah'. But that was only one part of the prophecy. The other was that he would prepare the way for Jesus. John preached a message of repentance and baptized those who rededicated their lives to God in the Jordan River. He also proclaimed that Jesus was the one who had come to bring salvation. The Apostle John wrote of the Baptizer: '... John saw Jesus coming toward him and said, "Look, the Lamb of God, who takes away the sin of the world! This is the one I meant when I said, 'A man who comes after me has surpassed me because he was before me." (1:29-30)

Without a doubt, John lived out the calling on his life. The one Gabriel announced to his father Zechariah when he shattered the silence. Let us reflect for a moment on the powerful message and imagery in Zechariah's story.

God has been **silent** for four hundred years. An angel tells him that his son will be the **Voice in the Wilderness**, but Zechariah cannot believe it. He is then struck **mute** until his son is born and he declares in **writing** that his name is John. This child does indeed grow up to be the **Voice of one calling** in the wilderness.

And the wilderness is a place of solitude and quiet. A place where a voice can be heard, and a place people would have to go on purpose. John's ministry wasn't just another voice in the noise of a crowded city, but an anointed calling to turn hearts back to God

Nothing is ever random with God, and we're going to see that even more clearly in the days and weeks ahead. As we uncover more details that testify to the irrefutable intentionality of God think of it as a heartbeat thrumming through the ages. The heartbeat of God revealed in his Word.

Dear Lord, thank you that even in seasons of silence, your promises are true. Forgive me for my unbelief as you forgave Zechariah. Remind me to daily come into your presence so I can have confidence like Gabriel. I praise you for second chances and that my moments of doubt do not have to define me. Give me the boldness to believe your words are true *and* to proclaim them to the world. In Jesus' name. Amen.

- Are there any prayers you've prayed for a long time? Have those prayers worn any holes in your faith?
- How can the consequences of sin cause stronger faith in God?
- Can you think of a time when God extended a second chance to you?

5) The Lord has Done This for Me

"'The Lord has done this for me,' she said.
"In these days he has shown his favor
and taken away my disgrace among the people.'"-- Luke 1:25

★ **Read Luke 1:24-25, 39-45**

Alright, now we're going to look at Elizabeth. After all, it's her story I started with. I've always liked her. She seems so down-to-earth. And she'd have to be to raise a child living in the spirit and power of Elijah!

The first recorded words we have from Elizabeth are ones of gratitude. She recognized that this pregnancy was only possible through God. We don't know how old she was, but she was certainly beyond natural child-bearing years. Menopause had come and gone. And then a baby was growing in her womb!

She spoke of God taking away her disgrace. Having children was everything in her culture. If a woman had many children, she was blessed by God. If a woman had no children, she was cursed by God. It was so important a man could actually divorce his wife for being barren. Imagine how hard it must have been for Elizabeth, particularly as a priest's wife, to go month after month with an empty womb. I struggled with infertility for two years before having my son. People would ask when we were having children and it was like a knife in my heart. I remember feeling broken. For Elizabeth, the stigma must have been crushing.

So, isn't it curious that she went into seclusion? She certainly wasn't ashamed of her pregnancy or trying to keep it a secret. She may have been seeking some insulation from prying eyes and the gossips with a thousand questions. In this current moment, our lives are so much on display in social media and maybe we could take a page from Elizabeth's playbook. Privacy can be a good thing. Quiet can be best.

What's more, I believe Elizabeth spent this time privately preparing her heart to become a mother. After all, she'd likely given up any real hope of it ever happening. And now she wasn't just going to be a mother, but the mama of the one who would prepare the way for the Lord. As we discussed with Zechariah, these are significant revelations. Zechariah and Elizabeth were ordinary people who lived in a little backwater town in Judea. Before Gabriel's announcement, they never expected to be people of any significance. After that, I imagine they spent a lot of time praying and trying to prepare for parenthood.

But Elizabeth wasn't left entirely by her lonesome during her pregnancy. She received a most special visitor—her cousin Mary. Now, it's possible I'm just a little dense but I had an 'aha' moment as I was studying and writing and working on this. It's doubtful Elizabeth even knew Mary was coming, and even more doubtful that she knew Mary had big news. No texts or video calls or even snail mail out here in the ancient hills. No, when Mary arrived at Elizabeth's doorstep—Elizabeth had no earthly idea that Mary was pregnant with the Promised One.

Until the baby leaped in her womb. John—already a little wild child—jumped in her belly at the sound of Mary's voice. Oh, those first kicks are amazing but this probably just about knocked Old Elizabeth over! And then, Elizabeth herself was filled with the Holy Spirit.

Friends, I could cry for her. This barren old woman filled with the Spirit and possibly the first person clued in on the best secret in all human history. People assumed her infertility was punishment for sin. They didn't know that it was all part of God's perfect timing. If God had answered Elizabeth and Zechariah's first prayers for a child, then their son would not have been able to prepare the way for Jesus. All those years of disappointment were heartbreaking and difficult. I don't want to gloss over the very real pain Elizabeth experienced. I think it makes her faith all the more precious. And now Elizabeth is filled not only physically in her womb with a growing baby but filled also with the Holy Spirit.

And then we see Elizabeth's sweet soul. Filled with the Spirit, she blessed and encouraged Mary, and affirmed the promises of God. She rejoiced in humility. Elizabeth could have questioned why a girl so young and inexperienced would be chosen as the mother of the Messiah, and why she would be given the 'lesser' blessing of carrying the Messiah's forerunner instead. If we're honest, often we look to the right and left and wonder why someone else is blessed in a way that we are not. We want their blessing. We think we deserve it. But Elizabeth was a woman of true humility. She was sincerely joyful for her young cousin's blessing and wanted to encourage her to believe the promise she'd been given. Her thoughts were not for herself but for God. And, by the way, this is exactly how John the Baptist was around Jesus. His thoughts were always for God's glory and not his own. The apple didn't fall far from the tree–Elizabeth taught her son well.

> "Those that are filled with the Holy Ghost have low thoughts of their own merits, and high thoughts of God's favors." – Matthew Henry

I want to close with one last thought. As I read through commentaries, this phrase penned by Matthew Henry resonated deeply with me: **"Believing souls are blessed souls, and will be found so at last."** He wrote this in response to verse 45 where Elizabeth said, "Blessed is she who has believed that the Lord would fulfill his promises to her!"

When I was in college, I picked one word to be my favorite word. It was the word 'Dickensian'. No, just kidding. It was 'believe'. You see, I had spent two or three years walking on a prodigal road. Looking for worth in every nook and cranny. Wanting to feel like I was wanted and loved. As an adult, I can see how many teens and young adults stumble along a similar path trying to find their identity in a world that's broken and dying. To be honest, I see a lot of grown adults still searching. Searching for something that tells them that who they are matters.

When the fragile world I built in my early twenties collapsed, I realized I had tried to build my life on things that would never hold. And yet, I wasn't quite like the foolish man who built his life upon the sand. I'll tell you why–I had a firm foundation. My building materials turned out to be shoddy, but my foundation was all I had left. That bedrock was believing in Jesus as the Son of God and my Savior. And it was enough.

> "Therefore everyone who hears these words of mine and puts them into practice is like a wise man who built his house on the rock. The rain came down, the streams rose, and the winds blew and beat against that house; yet it did not fall, because it had its foundation on the rock. But everyone who hears these words of mine and does not put them into practice is like a foolish man who built his house on sand. The rain came down, the streams rose, and the winds blew and beat against that house, and it fell with a great crash."–Matthew 7:24-27

'Believe' became my favorite word. When I had nothing else to hold onto, I could still believe in Jesus. When everything and everyone else let me down, I could still believe that Jesus loved me. When the circumstances of my life ebbed and flowed in and out of hardship, I could still believe in the sovereignty and plans of God. When life was dark and scary, I could still believe in the hope of an eternal future with no more pain or sorrow. 'Believe' carried me through the darkest nights of my soul, and will carry me through to the end.

Now, I hold to being authentic and vulnerable even when it doesn't look good on paper. I have struggled hard to hold onto my belief. Some struggles seemed to have naturally brought me closer to God; others have not. I've sometimes struggled to believe in the goodness and faithfulness of God. When it feels like I've carried too much for too long and my legs are buckling. In those seasons, it has been essential to hear and listen to voices that remind me to hold on. Voices like Elizabeth when she said to Mary: "...blessed is she who believed that what was spoken to her by the Lord would be fulfilled."

This humble, ordinary couple lived in confident faith. They raised their son in obedience to God's commands. Together they believed in the promises of God and worshiped him in the power of the Holy Spirit. They may have started as a childless old couple from a backwater town, but they proved to be just the right people to raise the Voice in the Wilderness.

Dear Lord, thank you for your gift of mercy. I praise you for the blessings that are poured out at just the right time, and for your sustaining love in disappointment. Strengthen my belief in your goodness. Help me to encourage one another in times of hardship. Thank you for always hearing the prayers of my heart. Amen.

- How do you respond when life takes a sudden turn? Is it natural to prioritize spending intentional time with God? Or does focusing on the details tend to take priority? Perhaps you try to ignore the problem altogether?
- Reflect on a season of difficulty that you have experienced. Did you, like me, struggle to believe in God's goodness? Or did it draw you closer to him? Who encouraged you in that season?
- Is there anyone you know currently going through something difficult? How can you be an encouragement to them?

6) Mary's Story

"For no word from God will ever fail."-- Luke 1:37

The night Jesus was born, I slept with my hand on his chest. Far from our home in Nazareth, in a little stable cave in Bethlehem. He was snug in swaddling cloths and he slept in a manger carved in the cave's wall. Me, I was completely exhausted, and resting as best I could. But I had to be near him. I had to keep one hand on him. I wanted to feel the warmth of his tiny body, the gentle rise and fall of his steady breathing. I needed to be near him. After all, I was his mother and he was my son. And although there was so much I didn't and couldn't understand, that much was perfectly clear to me. He was the Hope of the world, and I was his mother.

As I lay there with my hand on his tiny chest, the words of the angel washed over me again. I whispered them to myself and let my thoughts drift back to that day nine months earlier in Nazareth.

"Greetings, you who are highly favored! The Lord is with you."

I don't know that anyone who has ever actually encountered an angel has expected to, and even if they were expecting it, I doubt they were really prepared. As for me? I was terrified. And confused. I couldn't begin to fathom what he meant. How could I be highly favored? I was just a poor Jewish girl, a girl. No one I ever knew would call a woman highly favored by God. And besides, I wasn't anything special. Only an ordinary girl doing ordinary things. I didn't know what to say or even think, and I was more than a little afraid. What if this was no angel, but a deceitful spirit sent to ensnare me?

He must've sensed my confusion for then he said to me, **"Do not be afraid, Mary, you have found favor with God. You will be with child and give birth to a son, and you are to give him the name Jesus. He will be great and will be called the Son of the Most High. The Lord God will give him the throne of his father David, and he will reign over the house of Jacob forever; his kingdom will never end."**

The impact of these words hit me like a gust of wind, and I stumbled back. My hand covered my mouth as I tried to understand. That I should have a child? A child who will be called the Son of the Most High? Who will receive the throne of David? And reign over the house of Jacob forever? Oh, I might've just been a girl, but I knew the scriptures. I knew what was written and foretold. The covenants that carried my people through the ages. It was the greatest hope of every woman to be the mother of the Messiah! And that I should deliver this child?

A child. **"How can this be?"** I asked, a little breathless. **"I have not been intimate with a man."**

Gabriel explained gently, **"The Holy Spirit will come upon you, and the power of the Most High will overshadow you. Therefore the child to be born will be holy; he will be called the Son of God."**

It seemed to please the angel very much to talk about the Son of God. Now, this might seem irreverent, but I promise you: Gabriel grinned as he added, **"Even your relative Elizabeth has also become pregnant with a son in her old age—although she was called barren, she is now in her sixth month! For nothing is impossible with God."**

All my life, my mother and the other women have pitied and prayed for

Elizabeth. Her child-bearing years were long over. And now she was with child? Gabriel's words echoed in my mind and through my very heart. For nothing is impossible with God. His words are never powerless.

After all, this same God spoke all the world into being. This same God called Abraham and made him into a great nation. This same God delivered my people from Egypt. This same God provided manna and quail to my ancestors in the desert. This same God was with Sarah and Ruth and Esther. The God of Abraham, Isaac, and Jacob. My God.

I didn't have to understand everything to believe the angel's message. I only had to trust and obey God. It wouldn't be an easy path. The punishment for pregnancy before marriage was the same as that for adultery–death by stoning. Yet, if this was God's plan and I was the one he had chosen, then I had to trust that he would protect me. He would provide.

I nodded slowly as I squared my shoulders, **"I am the Lord's servant. May it be to me as you have said."**

I knew it would be hard. Didn't Abraham struggle? Didn't Moses have difficulty? Who was I to think my life would be any easier? But when the road got very hard I held on to what the angel told me: God is with you.

When Joseph looked so hurt and heartbroken and talked of divorce, I remembered that God was with me. I trusted he would show Joseph his plan. And he did. When people stared and whispered, I remembered that God was with me. Through everything, I held onto God's promise and a well of hope deep in my heart sustained me.

I decided to visit Elizabeth for a while, to get out of Nazareth and be with someone who would understand this miracle. When I called out to her, her baby jumped in her womb! Oh, how she laughed. It was the lightest, most joyful laugh I have ever heard. She was filled with the Holy Spirit and she called me 'blessed.' She knew! She knew before I even explained that I was carrying the Son of God. We grabbed hold of one another, hugging and crying. I put my hand on her growing belly, and she put her hand on mine, and together we rejoiced for the goodness of God.

I went home to Joseph just after John was born. I told Joseph how the house had been full of neighbors and relatives, how they had argued over the baby's name, and how Zechariah had praised God when his speech returned. Joseph praised God for this incredible miracle, and yet he seemed troubled. After all, the birth of our child would not be celebrated with all our neighbors and relatives. Most of them were hardly speaking to us. Everyone knew this child was conceived before he brought me home in marriage. The rumors still swirled, getting bigger as I did. My own parents didn't know what to think. I held onto the words from God that I was highly favored by him, but my friends and family were ashamed. Some days the only thing that held me together was the fragile bloom of hope I sheltered in my heart.

Then, the Emperor issued a census. Every head of household had to return to the city of his family's ancestry. Joseph belonged to the house and line of David—all the way in Bethlehem. And my time was coming ever closer.

We discussed what to do. We even argued a bit. Often switching sides halfway through! After all, Joseph didn't have to take me with him. The census did not require it. The journey would be difficult and hard. Sometimes I felt sure I could make it, and other times I was sure the lesser risk was delivering my child in Nazareth without him. But Joseph could never quite agree to that, knowing that without him I might be alone.

So, we decided to go together. And when the labor pains started, I was grateful for his strong hand to hold. Joseph was so level-headed and sure, even though I've always suspected he was more than a little scared. In a small cave in the City of David, Jesus was born. It was not what we planned. And yet, none of that mattered when I held him. My child. The Son of the Most High.

Joseph rustled up fresh hay to place in the manger–just a little stone trough carved into the side of the wall for the animals to feed. It would do. Oh, how we wanted to give him more. This baby deserved the best of everything, and we had nothing. Nothing but our love and our faithfulness and our commitment to do our best by God.

A baby wrapped in swaddling cloths and lying in a manger turned out to be the exact sign the angels gave the shepherds who came to worship Jesus. That very night. I remember looking at Joseph and his dark eyes were brimming with tears. God had brought people to celebrate the birth of his son–and our son. We were not alone. God was with us.

That night, when I laid down to rest, I knew that my hope was well placed. The angel, the miracle, the Son of the Most High, it was the very hand of God bringing forth salvation–for all of us. The Grace that had been bestowed upon me was now swaddled in a manger. The Hope of mankind sleeping in the dark. And when I laid my hand on his chest, I knew that the Light of the World had come into the world.

- How does the promise that 'God is with you' give you hope?
- What do you think was hardest for Mary in being Jesus's mother?

7) A Few Details

"In the sixth month of Elizabeth's pregnancy,
God sent the angel Gabriel to Nazareth, a town in Galilee,
to a virgin pledged to be married to a man named Joseph,
a descendant of David. The virgin's name was Mary." – Luke 1:26-27

Our text for today is the two verses printed above. We're going to dive deep into Luke's brief description of Mary and find hidden treasures in the scripture.

Let's start with her name. Mary. It's a variant of the Hebrew name 'Miriam'. Miriam was the sister of Moses and Aaron which harkens the imagination back to God's deliverance of his people from captivity in Egypt. The name 'Miriam' means 'exalted'. Biblical names are infused with rich symbolism. Mary's name reminds us of God's faithfulness to his people and reflects the favor she found with God.

Next, Luke noted that she was engaged or betrothed to a man named Joseph. We'll learn more about Jewish marriage customs when we read and reflect on Joseph's story. For now, it's important for us to understand that she was in a legally binding marriage contract with Joseph that could only be broken with a legal divorce.

When we read about Mary here in Luke 1:26-27, we see that her virginity is emphasized. We've gotten so used to the idea of the virgin birth that we gloss over this detail. Yet, Luke–the very guy who sometimes skimped on the details–gave us this one twice. Why is this so important? Let's look at another gospel writer for answers.

"This is how the birth of Jesus the Messiah came about: His mother Mary was pledged to be married to Joseph, but before they came together, she was found to be pregnant through the Holy Spirit...All this took place to fulfill what the Lord had said through the prophet: 'The virgin will conceive and give birth to a son, and they will call him Immanuel' (which means 'God with us')."-- Matthew 1:18, 22-23

Long before Mary was even born, the prophet Isaiah wrote that 'The virgin will conceive and give birth to a son, and will call him Immanuel.' (7:14) The name 'Immanuel' means 'God With Us'. This was just one of many prophecies that a Savior would come. For hundreds of years, the Jews have waited for their Savior to come. And wondered how a virgin could be his mother.

An argument has been made by skeptics that this verse in Isaiah is mistranslated, and instead of 'virgin' the word is 'maiden'. However, this is refuted by an important fact. A century or two before the birth of Jesus, Jewish scholars translated the scriptures from Hebrew to Greek. When they did this, they translated Isaiah 7:14 with a Greek word that unequivocally means 'virgin'. Therefore, we can know that their understanding of the verse was that a virgin would conceive.

One more bit of prophecy regarding the virgin birth, let's go all the way back to the beginning. In Genesis 3, Eve is tempted by the serpent to sin against God. When the serpent is cursed, God says:

"I will put animosity
  between you and the woman—
    between your seed and her seed.

He will crush your head,
and you will crush his heel." (TLV)

Throughout the rest of the Old Testament, 'seed' is associated with men–Abraham, Jacob, and David. Yet here at the Fall, God says it will be the woman's seed. A child conceived without a biological father, the one foretold in Isaiah 7:14.

Ever heard the saying 'The devil is in the details'? Yet, when we read about Mary we see that *God* is in the details. The hope of mankind is hidden in every detail. There is nothing random in the nativity story, no detail that was left to chance.

Okay, we still have a couple more details about Mary to uncover. We read in both Luke and Matthew that Mary (and Joseph) was a descendant of King David. When we turn in our Bibles to 2 Samuel 7:11-16 we read this promise:

'The Lord declares to you that the Lord himself will establish a house for you: When your days are over and you rest with your ancestors, I will raise up your offspring to succeed you, your own flesh and blood, and I will establish his kingdom. He is the one who will build a house for my Name, and I will establish the throne of his kingdom forever. I will be his father, and he will be my son. When he does wrong, I will punish him with a rod wielded by men, with floggings inflicted by human hands. But my love will never be taken away from him, as I took it away from Saul, whom I removed from before you. Your house and your kingdom will endure forever before me; your throne will be established forever.'

This is a huge promise! Unfortunately, it wasn't long after David's death that the kingdom of Israel was torn in two by civil war. More than that, the Jews became a conquered people–Babylonians, Greeks, Romans. When Gabriel came to speak to Mary, King Herod the Great was named 'King of the Jews'--but his lineage was Arabian and his family converted to Judaism during the time of the Maccabees in a bid for power. The Jewish people were waiting for God to keep this promise to David, but they were expecting a literal ruler. One who would overthrow the Romans and reign as David did in the glory days long ago.

> A covenant is a binding promise made between two parties. Throughout the Old Testament God made several covenants with individuals (Noah, Abraham, Moses, and David), and his people the Israelites. Jesus established a new covenant with his death and resurrection, and all are invited to enter into it.

This promise, which is known as the Davidic Covenant, is another prophecy concerning the Messiah. The one who will reign forever.

> "Of the greatness of his government and peace
> there will be no end.
> He will reign on David's throne
> and over his kingdom,
> establishing and upholding it
> with justice and righteousness
> from that time on and forever."
> –Isaiah 9:6-7

The reason Matthew and Luke give us the genealogies of Jesus is not because they had an awesome subscription to Ancestry.com. It's to verify the prophecy of the Davidic covenant's fulfillment in Jesus. Because Mary (and Joseph) was a descendant of David, her son can fulfill this prophecy.

Alright, last bit for today. Luke tells us that Mary lived in Nazareth. This is the first time Nazareth is mentioned, not only in the Bible but also in the Apocrypha and in the writings of the Jewish historian Josephus. Perhaps this is not so surprising when we stop to consider how unremarkable Nazareth was in the first century. It was a small little village nestled in the hills and about fifteen miles from the Sea of Galilee. No major roads went by Nazareth. A person only went there on purpose. The town was so small just one well, fed by a spring several miles away, provided water for the residents.

It was also an impoverished town. Under Roman oppression, most Jews lived at the poverty level. There is no question that Mary was anything other than a poor, ordinary Jewish girl living in a backwater town. Her biggest hope was to marry Joseph and carry on the traditions of their people. And yet, today, we've uncovered in just a few simple details how God's plan will unfold in Mary's life; how the promise to rescue mankind from the ravages of evil revealed to us through the prophets will be manifested through a humble virgin in a tiny town.

"The angel was sent to her from Nazareth. Note, No distance or disadvantage of place shall be a prejudice to those for whom God has favors in store. The angel Gabriel carries his message as cheerfully to Mary and Nazareth in Galilee as to Zacharias in the temple at Jerusalem."--Matthew Henry

Dear Lord, thank you for the gift of your Word. For the promises that have stood for generations and are fulfilled in Jesus, and Jesus alone. Let the hope of the gospel wash over us this Christmas. Help us to remember in all our details and planning, that you planned the details for our rescue before time began. There is nothing random in your salvation story. Amen.

- Mary's society shut her out. Can you recall a time when you felt shut out by your friends and family? What did you do to keep from despair? How did God lead you through?
- When circumstances in your own life don't match up with what God has promised, how do you react? How can you hold onto hope in hard times?
- Are there times when Jesus wasn't what you were expecting? Was there ever a time when Jesus met you in your circumstances, and offered relationships instead of actually changing your circumstances?
- Are there details in your story that you would rewrite? Circumstances you would change? How can God use those details to bring glory to himself through your life?
- Pain like this seems to be especially hard at Christmastime. How can you reach out to someone who is experiencing the pain of isolation, or difficult circumstances?

8) The Annunciation

"I am the Lord's servant," Mary answered.
"May your word to me be fulfilled."-- Luke 1:38

★ **Read Luke 1:28-38**

Today we're going to spend time in more familiar territory. In fact, here is where we can pick up our cherished old quilt and look at the threads of the most careworn places of the Christmas story. As we settle into Mary's story, let's look for truths in the stitching we have never noticed before.

Luke told us exactly what Zechariah was doing when Gabriel appeared, he does not give us the same details about Mary. Legend has imagined her at a well, weaving cloth, or reading a book (which is impossible since books didn't exist in that format in her time). I have to assume it doesn't really matter what she was doing. Perhaps the reason we were told about Zechariah is to underscore his disbelief. This priest offering incense and prayers in the Temple in Jersualem couldn't believe an angel. This young peasant woman doing something so ordinary it doesn't bear mentioning had a different response. Let's lean in and hear what it was.

When Gabriel appeared and greeted her, he told her she had found favor with God. Luke tells us that Mary was 'greatly troubled at his words'. I can think of three reasons why Mary would've been distressed at this greeting.

1. We usually imagine that angels are really pretty or look like cute babies or something incredibly harmless. The fact is, every time someone in the Bible saw an angel, the first thing the angel had to

say was 'do not be afraid!' Perhaps in part, it's simply startling to be accosted by an angelic being, but there's also something over-aweing about angels.

2. On top of that, this angel is giving Mary a high compliment. One she would never expect as a poor, ordinary Jewish girl. Women were second-class citizens in Mary's day, but women were part of God's redemptive plan.

3. Mary was a humble person. In fact, every commentary I read remarked on the humility of Mary. She would never have imagined such an encounter or such a compliment from an Angel of the Most High.

Gabriel, bless him, saw her fear and gave the typical 'do not be afraid' line. And then, did you notice he called her by name? Mary. I love this little detail. God didn't just point his messenger in the right direction and say 'Go tell that girl this thing.' Gabriel knew her by name. This was personal. And I have to think that it heartened Mary. What's more, is that we can take heart because God calls us by name as well. Check out this verse in Isaiah: 'But now, this is what the LORD says— he who created you, Jacob, he who formed you, Israel: "Do not fear, for I have redeemed you; I have summoned you by name; you are mine."' (43:1)

Gabriel went on to lay it all out there for Mary: she was to conceive, but not just any ordinary child. The Son of the Most High. Then he referenced two covenants. The first one with David we already discussed. Let's look at the second one in the phrase 'he will reign over Jacob's descendants forever.'

To dig into this, I want to use the Tree of Life translation of the Bible. Messianic Rabbi Jason Sobel explains, "The Tree of Life Version speaks with a decidedly Jewish-friendly voice—a voice like the Bible authors themselves—to recover the authentic context of the Scriptures and biblical faith." Let's read Genesis 28:13-15 in the TLV together.

> Surprisingly, Adonai was standing on top of it and He said, "I am Adonai, the God of your father Abraham and the God of Isaac. The land on which you lie, I will give it to you and to your seed. Your seed will be as the dust of the land, and you will burst forth to the west and to the east and to the north and to the south. And in you all the families of the earth will be blessed—and in your seed. Behold, I am with you, and I will watch over you wherever you go, and I will bring you back to this land, for I will not forsake you until I have done what I promised you."

Did you catch the promise here—the one that relates to Mary? God promises Jacob that through his seed, or offspring, all families on earth will be blessed. Remember the curse of the serpent in Genesis 3—the seed of the woman will crush his head. These verses connect and find fulfillment in Mary's son Jesus as Gabriel revealed to Mary. He is the one through whom all families on earth will be blessed, and he is the one who will crush the serpent's head, and he is the one who will reign forever in a kingdom with no end.

Let's not rush through this beautiful truth. In 1 Corinthians 15 we read, 'For since death came through a man, the resurrection of the dead comes also through a man. For as in Adam all die, so in Christ all will be made alive.' Adam introduced sin and death to mankind, and Jesus is our *only* redemption. Through him, and him alone, we have eternal life.

42

But in Mary, we also have something of a second Eve. The name Eve means 'life' or 'living' because she is the mother of all the living. It is through her that salvation was promised–her seed, her offspring. Mary herself could not redeem us, but she, like Eve, had a choice to make. She had to choose to submit to God's plan or to reject it. Eve rejected God's will for her life when she was tempted by the serpent. Mary, however, submitted to God's plan though it would come at a high cost.

> Scan this QR code for an article from Plough Magazine about a piece of art simply titled 'Mary and Eve'. It is a beautiful piece of art, rich with meaning and symbolism.

Now let's consider Mary's response. At first glance, it doesn't seem that different from Zechariah. However, Zechariah asked how he could be *sure*. He was asking for further proof. The word of an angel alone was not enough for him, and boy, did he get it! Yet Mary asked how this '*will*' be'. She was already believing and affirming the word she received, even though the logistics were beyond her.

Gabriel explained that the Holy Spirit would come upon Mary, and the power of the Most High would overshadow her. When we read about Elizabeth we discussed how the experience of the Holy Spirit was different prior to the ascension of Jesus. We saw how the Spirit enabled Elizabeth to have understanding and to speak blessings. Here, we see a very different function of the Holy Spirit–that of a hovering cloud which is the presence and power of God. This imagery is found throughout the Old Testament.

- In the beginning God created the heavens and the earth. Now the earth was formless and empty, darkness was over the surface of the deep, and the Spirit of God was hovering over the waters. –Genesis 1:1-2

- By day the Lord went ahead of them in a pillar of cloud to guide them on their way and by night in a pillar of fire to give them light, so that they could travel by day or night.--Exodus 13:21

- Then the angel of God, who had been traveling in front of Israel's army, withdrew and went behind them. The pillar of cloud also moved from in front and stood behind them, coming between the armies of Egypt and Israel. Throughout the night the cloud brought darkness to the one side and light to the other side; so neither went near the other all night long...During the last watch of the night the Lord looked down from the pillar of fire and cloud at the Egyptian army and threw it into confusion.--Exodus 14:19-20, 24

- When the priests withdrew from the Holy Place, the cloud filled the temple of the Lord. And the priests could not perform their service because of the cloud, for the glory of the Lord filled his temple. Then Solomon said, "The Lord has said that he would dwell in a dark cloud; I have indeed built a magnificent temple for you, a place for you to dwell forever."-- 1 Kings 8:11-13

- While he [Peter] was still speaking, a bright cloud covered them, and a voice from the cloud said, "This is my Son, whom I love; with him I am well pleased. Listen to him!" When the disciples heard this, they fell facedown to the ground, terrified.--Matthew 17:5-6

This is just a sampling of the passages I found where the Spirit is depicted as a cloud. Throughout Exodus, Leviticus, Numbers, and Deuteronomy the Israelites repeatedly experienced the presence of God as an overpowering cloud. However, this was not just a one-time deal for that generation. The Spirit appeared again in this way at the dedication of the temple in Jerusalem, and the prophet Ezekiel similarly saw the Spirit leave the temple in a vision. The last time we see the Spirit manifest as a cloud is at the transfiguration of Jesus.

> "This cloud was a visible manifestation of the glory and presence of God; this means that the same power of God that was with Moses and others in the Old Testament was now going to do a unique work in the life of Mary."-- David Guzik

We no longer have to experience the Holy Spirit this way—in a cloud that frankly seems terrifying at times. The Spirit dwells *within* us so that we are never without the presence of God. The power that through the Word brought all creation into being, the power that supernaturally protected the Israelites from the Egyptian army, and the power that caused a young virgin to conceive a child is living and active within us. The cool takeaway here? Whatever God has said he will do, he will do through the power of his Spirit. Like Mary, we need only to believe and submit to his plans. Mary didn't have to figure out how to conceive God's son on her own. That surely would have been impossible!

As if highlighting the miraculous power of the God he serves, Gabriel told Mary that Elizabeth was pregnant. I can almost see her mouth drop as she realized Gabriel's meaning. Only a miracle could allow Elizabeth to be pregnant. There are echoes in Elizabeth's pregnancy of the patriarchs who miraculously conceived in the scriptures; Abraham and Sarah, Isaac and

Rebekah, Jacob and Rachel. How Mary's imagination must have swirled as she absorbed the words of Gabriel.

Then, the very last thing Gabriel said to Mary is our premise statement for this whole book: 'For nothing is impossible with God' or 'No word of God will ever fail.' Again, God's word echoes through the ages. In Genesis 18, Abraham and Sarah are promised a son, but Sarah laughs. She is pushing ninety and cannot fathom such a thing is possible. The Angel of the Lord replies, 'Is anything too hard for the Lord?'

And now Gabriel waited for Mary's response. Luke doesn't tell us what she was thinking or feeling. Only that she answered, "I am the Lord's servant. May your word to me be fulfilled."

It's such a simple statement, isn't it? Just this one sentence. I wonder how long Gabriel waited for her answer. You don't get the feeling it was a long time (a pregnant pause, if you will). In my Sunday School class, we've been doing a study on faith. A point we've discussed time and again is what it looks like to be tested. At this moment, Mary was facing a test: would she trust God and submit to his plans? Or would she reject his plans because she is afraid? Unwilling? Unbelieving? God knew what she would choose, but Mary didn't. God knows all of us better than we know ourselves. Often, it is through testing that we discover deeper wells of faith than we knew we had.

And because I'm such a geek for words, let me point out exactly what Mary said: "Let this happen to me according to your *word*." It's so good, isn't it?

Dear God, I thank you that nothing is impossible for you. Jesus, I praise you as the unfailing Word. Spirit, I thank you for being living

and active within me, and I don't have to do anything in my own strength. Help me to submit as Mary did with humility and faith. Amen.

- We can see through Mary that God works through our doubts and questions—even when they go unspoken. Can you think of a time when you were hesitant or had questions about doing God's will?
- What kind of answers do we give to God? Are we always willing to do his commands? To trust his plans? What would it look like to live as faith-filled as Mary?
- The Holy Spirit is present in every believer. Do you live in the reality of this truth? Or do you try to do all things in your own power and understanding? If I'm honest–I live like it's all on me, even though I say it's all in God's control. How about you?

9) The Magnificat

'And Mary said: "My soul glorifies the Lord
and my spirit rejoices in God my Savior..."-- Luke 1:46-47

★**Read Luke 1:39-56**

Now let's revisit Mary's visit with Elizabeth. We looked at this before with our lens focused on Elizabeth. Today we're going to adjust our lens in Mary's direction.

There's no evidence that shows Mary shared her divine encounter and calling with anyone in Nazareth. We know nothing of her parents and their reaction to her pregnancy. In Elizabeth, Mary had a trusted friend with shared experience. Although it is certain that Mary believed and obeyed, I imagine that there were times of bewilderment. Elizabeth's Spirit-filled blessing must have been such a balm for her young heart. God truly was with her–and he provided companionship for the journey.

The ancient Celts had the phrase 'anam cara' which means 'soul-friend'. The anam cara was someone to whom you could share all your deepest secrets, your fears and failures, your hopes and joys. The soul friend was a companion and counselor. These beautiful, intimate friendships pointed one another to God and reflected the intimacy we are invited into with Jesus.

I know that soul friends are few and far between. Particularly now when we live such fast-paced lives. The feeling of isolation is quite high and reflected in the statistics of rising anxiety and depression. My friends, friendship is important. We see here in Luke 1 that God provided Elizabeth and Mary with friendship in their shared experience. I encourage you to pray for friendship and to look for ways to be a friend. And don't be surprised if God provides someone unexpected.

Elizabeth and Mary were very different. Elizabeth was old; Mary was young. Elizabeth waited for her baby for a long, long time; Mary was completely surprised to find out she'd have a baby before she was even married. Both women had reason to be nervous and afraid, but they were joyful and hopeful. They trusted God to keep his promises and to sustain them through difficulties. This friendship must have been such a source of strength for both of them.

The longest recorded words of Mary is a song of praise. This passage is referred to as 'The Magnificat' because of the Latin translation of the first line: Magnificat anima mea Dominum (my soul glorifies the Lord). Her song contains echoes of praises from past generations of faithful women and men. Scholars have asserted that this means Mary was a devout Jew who knew her scriptures well. I agree with them. I also believe it means that there are threads of praise that connect all of us who call upon the name of the Lord and rejoice in his faithfulness.

I've wrestled with just how deep to dive into this well (it's pretty deep) and how exactly the succinctly present the information (since it is Christmas and you may have cookies starting to burn in the oven). I'm gonna go with a list again. Sound good?

The Magnificat Trail

- The first stop is in **1 Samuel 2:1-10.**

  This is a song of praise from a woman named Hannah. Hannah
  struggled for years to conceive a child. She pleaded with God and
  promised to dedicate him to the Lord. After God blessed her with a
  child, she left her boy Samuel under the care of the priest Eli. Her
  son grew up to become a priest and prophet. He anointed King
  David. I've often thought of Hannah and Elizabeth together. The
  desires of their heart were delayed until just the right time–Samuel
  to anoint the greatest (earthly) king of Israel and John to prepare
  the way for the King of Kings. Mary's Magnificat is quite similar to
  Hannah's song of praise. Although their pregnancies were
  drastically different, both reflected the favor and power of the
  Lord.

- Next stop, **Psalm 113.**

  Psalm 113 is part of a set of psalms used during Passover known as
  the Egyptian Hallel. The Hebrew phrase 'Hallelu Yah' is used
  frequently throughout Psalm 113-118. The phrase means 'praise
  the Lord' and is where we get the transliterated word 'hallelujah'.
  Psalm 113 is read before the beginning of the Passover Seder. The
  imagery draws from Hannah's song of praise in 1 Samuel 2. This
  psalm would have been sung again and again by Mary during the
  Jewish feasts, particularly Passover. And Jesus sang it with the
  disciples at the Last Supper– Jesus, the lamb of God who takes
  away the sins of the world.

- In **Luke 1:49** Mary called God the 'Mighty One' (though, it's
  possible your translation may say something different but similar).

This is the only time God is called 'Mighty One' in the New Testament. Yet, when I popped the phrase into Bible Hub to see where else it comes up, I found dozens of usages in the Old Testament–Joshua, Isaiah, the Psalms. The phrase is used with warrior imagery, with God strong and mighty in battle.

- "He has performed mighty deeds with his arm."-- **Luke 1:51**
  The imagery of God's mighty arm, or righteous right hand, and so on is seen throughout the Old Testament. First and foremost, it is connected with God's deliverance of his people from Egypt. Although Mary is using language from her people's ancient past, she is speaking of God's activity unfolding in real-time. God was moving through Mary to deliver his people, indeed, to deliver all mankind once and for all.

- Read **Psalm 110:10** and **Psalm 103:17-18**
  In the midst of all this warrior imagery, Mary recalled that God is merciful to those who love him and fear him. This fear is one of awe, reverence, and humility before the Mighty One. The One who saves will rescue those who call on him.

- Okay, we're on the last stop of the Magnificat trail, **Isaiah 41:8-10.** Mary wraps up her song of praise with echoes of the prophet Isaiah, who in turn was calling on the promises God made to the patriarchs. We keep running into the promise God made when he cursed the serpent that Eve's Seed would crush his head, and that through Abraham, Isaac, and Jacob all nations will be blessed. The rivers of God's narrative come together in these beautiful estuaries of promise and hope. And in Mary's song, there is an outpouring of praise. Also, did you catch Isaiah's use of the phrase 'righteous right hand'?

Over and over again in Scripture, I see God's people telling their history back to themselves. They remind one another of what God has already done. We do this today too. When we remember what God has already done it gives us hope and strength as we wait on his promises. We would be wise to be like Mary; to praise God for the mercy and grace he is showing us right now, to reflect on his faithfulness through the ages, and to look forward to the fulfillment of all his promises with joy and hope. Jesus is coming again. The Mighty One will rescue us with his strong arm–forever.

Holy Father in Heaven, the stories of your faithfulness speak from across the ages. Give me words to carry the stories forward, and to add my own as I share the good news of your Mighty Arm. Amen.

- Do you have a friend you are particularly connected to through a shared experience? How does that friendship help sustain you in hard times? How does your friendship reflect God's love and companionship?
- If someone was documenting your story, would there be more words of praise or worries? Write your own 'Magnifcat'. It can be long or short, so long as it is a song of praise. Like Mary, you can include imagery and stories from the ancient past. Or you can use the details of God's faithfulness from your own life story.

10) Joseph's Story

But after he had considered this, an angel of the Lord appeared to him
in a dream and said, "Joseph son of David, do not be afraid
to take Mary home as your wife, because what is conceived in her
is from the Holy Spirit.-- Matthew 1:20

It's important to me to do the right thing. Not necessarily the easy thing, or the simplest thing, but the right thing. The righteous thing. I've always wanted to be like King David, I suppose–a man after God's own heart. Maybe even a friend of God. But who am I? I'm just a craftsman from nowhere. Not a king or a warrior, not a prophet or a poet. I'm just a guy who works hard and tries to do the right thing.

And that's why I really had no idea what to do when Mary told me her, um, news. I wasn't prepared for it at all. To be a father before I became a husband? No, that was not the right thing. That's not how things are done.

Looking back, I can remember exactly how I felt when Mary told me she was pregnant. My cheeks flushed with anger–and confusion, hurt, betrayal, jealousy. Then, she explained the child was the Messiah, the son of God, the one we've been waiting for. My chest went so tight I couldn't breathe. I remember I grabbed the work table in my shop to steady myself. This story was incredible, impossible. Yet I trusted Mary to be an honest woman. Faithful and true, someone who would do the right thing. Like me.

I felt confused. I felt lost. I felt...afraid. To be honest, maybe I was afraid more than anything else. Afraid I'd been wrong about her, afraid of what people would think and say, afraid that I would look like a fool, and afraid of what would be done to Mary once her condition was discovered.

I prayed and prayed and prayed. Although, I must admit, I wasn't listening for God's answer. I was too upset. I could only pray again and again. And think. My mind raced. I considered the situation from every angle.

Just before I fell asleep that night, I decided there was only one thing to do–divorce Mary quietly. Divorce her before she was ever fully my wife. Cut ties with the woman I had planned to build a life with. I like plans–plans help me with each piece I craft. But I had no plan for this and the only right thing seemed to break away from Mary as discreetly as possible.

My chest was still unbearably tight when I fell asleep that night. That I slept at all was a mercy from God. But when the angel came to me in a dream, he told me everything I needed to know: **"Joseph, son of David, do not be afraid to take Mary as your wife, because the child conceived in her is from the Holy Spirit. She will give birth to a son and you will name him Jesus, because he will save his people from their sins."**

He called me 'son of David.' Me–the guy who always wanted to be just a little like King David, a guy after God's own heart. Being in the line of David was, of course, very important to my family but I had never considered being called by that name.

He told me not to be afraid. He assured me her story was true–and that she was true. He told me I would name this son that she would deliver Jesus–Yeshua. It's a word that means to rescue, to save, to deliver. The one my wife would deliver was sent to deliver us.

When I awoke, I didn't feel afraid anymore.

Okay, well, let me be perfectly clear–I was afraid, but it was different. I was no longer afraid of what people would think or how I would look. And I wasn't afraid of what they'd do to Mary because I wasn't going to let anyone do anything to her. No, over my dead body would anyone harm a hair on her head. Instead, I was afraid, or perhaps a better word, overwhelmed with the enormity of what was unfolding in my life. I'm just a regular guy from nowhere. I do an honest business and try to live an honest life. And now the son of the Most High God was growing in my fiancé's womb? I was going to be some kind of father to the Messiah?

That fear kept me on my knees throughout all of Mary's pregnancy. I brought her home as my wife right away. It was the right thing to do. And we often talked about the future, trying to make sense of what we'd been told and what was happening right before our eyes. As Mary grew in size with every passing month, there was no way to doubt the message we'd been given. Yet we often wondered if we were equipped for the task ahead. Parenthood is a complex journey as it is. Children are almost never how you imagine them, and the experience of raising them is certainly nothing like you think it will be. How in the world could simple folks like us raise the King of Kings?

By faith. It was all I had. And it was enough.

We reminded each other again and again that God had chosen us. Chosen us, out of all people in all time. And if he chose us, he'd help us and he'd keep his promises–just as he had with Abraham and Moses and David and Esther. At night, when we couldn't sleep, we'd repeat the history of our people and travel those ancient pathways of God's faithfulness. Then, peace would come and we could rest knowing that God had a plan he would see through to completion. We were the tools he chose to use.

When the census was announced, I had no choice but to travel to Bethlehem. The Roman government did not care if a Jewish carpenter's wife was nearing the end of her pregnancy. Rome, after all, is ruthlessly efficient. I couldn't leave Mary alone and yet bringing her with me seemed reckless. In the end, we made the journey together. By faith.

Bethlehem was ill-equipped to handle the crowds. The inns were overflowing with people, and there was certainly nothing private available. When Mary's labor pains began, I had the horrifying thought that she might deliver in a crowded, noisy room full of strangers, or even worse–on the street. I begged, I harassed, I pleaded. Finally, a keeper of an inn found a place for us–in his stable. A small, cool cave for the livestock.

My first choice? Of course not. But there was privacy and clean straw, and the animals didn't seem to mind. And sometimes you don't get to be picky about the Lord's provisions. When God provided manna and quail to my ancestors in the wilderness, it was enough. And this stable was enough. Looking back, it may have been the most peaceful spot in all of Bethlehem that night.

I remember how his first cry sounded in that little cave. People expect me to tell them he sounded like an angel singing or something supernatural. But he sounded just like a baby. A baby shocked by the chill of this world, a baby already needing comfort from his mother's warmth and softness. Jesus, I have to tell you, was helpless and needy and fussy...and loud.

We swaddled him and after Mary nursed him we laid him in a little stone manger with clean straw. I stared at him for ages, trying to wrap my head around all the things I knew were true and reconcile them to this infant. This infant who needed me. The son of God needed...me.

I looked at Mary and Jesus, and my chest tightened again. Not with fear but with the burning desire to do right by them. And to do right by God. And I knew I had no special skills or experience to offer– but I had this desire and my faith in God to guide me. With His provision and protection, it would be enough. God himself thought it would be enough too.

When the Magi from the East came to worship Jesus, King Herod became aware of my son. He wanted to kill him because he was called 'the king of the Jews'. In another dream, I was told to take Mary and Jesus to Egypt. When I look back, again I feel the fear that gripped me–what if I failed? But my fear drove me closer to the Lord. My fear pushed me deeper into faith. I had to trust Him. And I had to obey.

We lived in Egypt until King Herod the Great died, but I was warned in another dream to take my family to Nazareth. This would be the safest place for Jesus to grow up. I grew up in Nazareth, as did Mary. And we knew that it was an obscure little village. It didn't seem like the kind of place to raise the Son of God. Shouldn't he be in Jerusalem? Somewhere important? Not pathetic little Nazareth with only the reputation that nothing good could come from there?

Yet, God provided the stable and God provided Nazareth. I knew I had to trust Him. We returned to Nazareth, to family and old friends, and settled into our lives as best we could. As a Jewish father, I was expected to teach my son the Torah and the ways of God. I had to model what it meant to be a righteous man. There could never be a more humbling experience. Raising children to fear and obey the Lord brings a man to his knees anyway. Raising Jesus? All I could do is trust the Lord to show me what was right, and then do it as best I could.

When all is said and done, I suppose I've done it—lived as a righteous man, maybe even become a friend of God. I know I'm the only man to have ever looked into the eyes of the Messiah and be called father. What a gift and honor from Adonai.

- I wonder if Joseph felt like literally running away as he considered what to do about Mary. Have you ever gone through an experience when you wanted to disappear? Did you handle your situation the way God wanted you to? How did you determine what to do?
- Joseph is usually just thought of as the silent step/foster father of Jesus, but he was so much more than that. List some of the interactions that Joseph would've had with Jesus. How do you think Joseph felt as he raised Jesus?

11) Upside Down

When Joseph woke up, he did what the angel of the Lord had commanded
him and took Mary home as his wife.-- Matthew 1:24

★**Read Matthew 1:18-25, 2:1-23**

"If a type is to be sought in the character of Joseph, it is that of a simple,
honest, hard-working, God-fearing man, who was possessed of large
sympathies and a warm heart. Strict in the observance of Jewish law and
custom, he was yet ready when occasion arose to make these subservient to
the greater law of the Spirit...Joseph is known to us only as a dim figure in the
background of the Gospel narratives, yet his whole-hearted reconciliation to
Mary, even in the face of possible slanderings by his neighbors, his complete
self-sacrifice, when he left all and fled into Egypt to save the infant Jesus, are
indicative that he was not unworthy to fulfill the great trust which was
imposed upon him by the Eternal Father."-- James Orr

I have always liked Joseph. Although we know very little about him, he was
clearly a God-fearing man of integrity and compassion. The first time we
see him in Scripture, we find him wrestling with a difficult decision. Joseph
was betrothed to Mary, and she became pregnant.

To fully understand the depth of this situation, let's look at the Jewish
marriage customs of the first century. There's a stark contrast to our own.

There were three phases to a Jewish engagement.
1. Engagement: Marriages were arranged between fathers. This
    match-making could take place in childhood, or closer to marrying

age. It was thought that young people didn't have the wisdom to make good marriage choices.

2. Betrothal/espousal/pledged: A period of up to one year following vows where the couple was legally bound to one another, but the marriage had not been consummated. At this point, divorce was required if the groom had second thoughts. Additionally, pregnancy before marriage was the same as adultery in the eyes of the law. The punishment for adultery was stoning.

3. Marriage: Within the year, the groom would come for his bride, their marriage could be consummated, and life together would begin.

One more historical detail here, it was quite common for marriages to take place when the bride and groom were sixteen or seventeen years old. The average lifespan was around twenty-nine years. Now, this piece of data is a little misleading. Childhood survival rates were very, very low. This brings the entire life expectancy average down. It makes sense that they would marry at a younger age in order to increase their child-bearing years and have children that survive into adulthood.

"Overall, science has generally concluded that if someone in the ancient world survived into adulthood and avoided wars and plagues, they could expect to live at least into their sixties."--Father Charles Grondin

So, although Mary and Joseph were betrothed they were as good as married in the eyes of the law, and the stakes were quite high. There's a tenderness in Joseph's decision to divorce Mary quietly. He was hoping to avoid drawing any attention to her, and thus spare her life.

After the angel appeared in his dream, Joseph had a new choice to make—obey God and bring Mary home as his wife; or continue with his own plan. Joseph obeyed. Matthew doesn't indicate that there was a significant length of time between Joseph waking up and his following through with what he had been told to do. Legally they were already bound in marriage, the last step was for Joseph to bring Mary home as his wife. And that's exactly what he did. Without delay.

Joseph trusted God. His faith wasn't in himself or in Mary, but in God. On his own, Joseph didn't know what to think or what to do! But as he trusted in God, he could walk in obedience and know that God would take care of all the details. Isn't his integrity and his trust in God just beautiful?

Sometimes it's hard to know what the right thing is to do. Sometimes trusting and obeying God can lead us into murky waters. Often I catch myself privately believing that if my goal is to be a good Christian God will just bless all the drama and difficulty right out of my way. Let me tell you, I don't know that I can say that has ever happened. And it certainly didn't happen for Joseph.

When Joseph trusted God, his world turned upside down. Let's consider his story:
- He married a pregnant woman which I am sure came with many sidelong glances. Perhaps it even hurt his business—reputation is everything in small towns. (Matt 1:24)

- Although newly married, he didn't consummate his marriage until after the birth of Jesus. This is a detail I blush to mention, but I think it's worth noting since it is another way in which Joseph's expectations must've gone a little sideways. (Matt 1:25)

- Joseph took his heavily pregnant wife with him to Bethlehem for the census. It's tempting to think that Caesar Augustus caused this, but it was foretold by the prophet Micah that the savior would be born in Bethlehem. (Luke 2:1-5; Micah 5:2)

- He became the stepfather/foster father to the Son of God. Can you imagine? When I really let that hit me, it's staggering. (Matt 1:26, Luke 2:6-7).

- Although Scripture doesn't explicitly tell us, it seems likely that Joseph set up shop in Bethlehem. We can infer from the Magi and Herod's edict that they followed the 'Bethlehem Star' for possibly two years. Joseph must have started up a business in Bethlehem, or the star would have led them to Nazareth instead. (Matt 2:1, 7-9)

- He had to lead his family forty miles from Bethlehem to Egypt to escape the murderous rampage of a dangerous king. Experts estimate this journey could have taken them three days! Matthew also notes that this was foretold by the prophet Hosea. (Matt 2:13-15, Hosea 11:1)

- Once Herod died, Joseph brought his family back to his hometown–Nazareth in Galilee. Back to the place where his story began. I wonder if it was hard to come home after many years away. Were the people welcoming? Or wary of the carpenter who had taken refuge in Egypt with his wife and illegitimate son? In any case, it meant starting over again for Joseph. (Matt 2:19-23).

It comforts me to know that I'm in good company when my world turns upside down, or life takes a sideways slide. Joseph experienced many life-altering changes. I've noticed that when hardship strikes, there's a tendency to think it must be punishment for sin. However, an overview of Joseph's story refutes that theory quite easily. To be sure, Joseph faced many difficulties *because* of his obedience to God–difficulties in which God sustained him, provided for him, and loved him. God equipped Joseph as he walked in obedience. These hardships were allowed, sometimes to fulfill prophecy, and the fruit was greater faith produced in Joseph.

Joseph's legacy of trust and obedience is only possible because of God. Without God, Joseph's entire life story would have looked quite different. If he had decided to divorce Mary and wash his hands of the whole ordeal, maybe he wouldn't have had to set up shop several times and flee to Egypt in fear of a mad king–but what blessings he would have forgone.

> Consider this quote as it applies to Joseph as well as Mary. "Often a work of God comes with two edges, great joy and great pain, and in that matter-of-fact response Mary embraced both. She was the first person to accept Jesus on his own terms, regardless of the personal cost." –Philip Yancey

My friends, we crave the easy life, don't we? Over the last few years, everyone I talk to remarks on how hard life seems to be. It's not even one crisis after another, but several at the same time. It feels crushing sometimes. And it's hard. I'm not dismissing that. Personally, my husband and I have walked through seasons of testing where our circumstances crowd in around us like rough bullies. We have often not known what the right thing is to do, and we have not been able to see the path before us. There have been times when I have shaken my fist toward heaven and demanded he do better. There have been other times when I have waited in stillness for God to move. I can assure you that God has loved me and sustained me in those seasons of quiet trusting and in those seasons of angry frustration. His plans have continued to unfold in my life, and he has continued to show more of himself to me.

You see, God shows up in the hard. We are not left alone to figure it out for ourselves. And when life is hard because we are obeying him, you can be sure he is there with us. When you do the honest thing at work, even if it costs you. When you parent differently, even though it's exhausting to choose the gentle way. When you follow your convictions, even though you face rejection. God is with us. Remember that was why Jesus came in the first place–he was Emmanuel, God with us. And when he returned to heaven, he promised we would not be left alone and sent the Holy Spirit to be with us in his stead.

Dear Lord, I may face impossible difficulties sometimes; but nothing is impossible with you. There were many times when the road ahead of Joseph was uncertain and difficult, but you were faithful to provide and sustain him. I trust you will do the same for me. I thank you and praise you for your faithfulness. Amen

- Think about times of testing in your own life. What was the choice you faced? What did you learn about yourself through it? What did you learn about God?
- What kind of difficulties are you facing right now? How is God there with you in the midst of those hardships? If you cannot see him, just ask. He'll show you his goodness.

12) The Name of Jesus

"She will give birth to a son, and you are to give him the name Jesus, because he will save his people from their sins."-- Matthew 1:21

When Gabriel appeared to Joseph he told him what to name the son Mary would deliver: Jesus. The name that's become so familiar to us is the Greek version of the name Yeshua, which means 'Yahweh is the Savior'. Another form of the name is Joshua.

Joshua is, of course, a book in the Old Testament. It recounts the battles of the Israelites led by Joshua as they reclaimed the Promised Land. Fourteen-hundred years before the birth of Jesus the Israelites experienced the saving power of Yahweh in the exodus from Egypt, his provision in the desert, and now in the conquering of many peoples in their pursuit of the Promised Land. Joshua's courage and might in battle and his strong leadership ability reflected the meaning of his name.

In the first century, Jesus/Yeshua was a common name among Jews. The historian Josephus names twelve of them in his historical records. The Jews were longing for the promised Messiah to deliver them from Rome, as Yahweh had delivered them from the oppression of the Egyptians.

Gabriel told Joseph the reason for the name Jesus was a little different than political deliverance. Instead, he said the reason was that he would 'save his people from their sins'. God's plans were bigger than his people imagined because their problem was bigger than they realized.

Then, as now, people lived as slaves to sin. Separated from God, their lives were defined by spiritual darkness. Fear crowded out hope. Despair drowned out peace. The oppression the Jews experienced under Rome paled in comparison to the oppression they experienced under Satan. And we experience it as well. There's a devouring darkness that seeks to destroy. We need a hero (cue the 80s song).

But Jesus didn't come as a conquering hero. This time. That's for next time; his second coming which you and I are awaiting today. No, in the incarnation Jesus came as a helpless infant. He lived as a poor tradesman and a nomadic teacher.

He appeared as a completely ordinary man and lived like one too.

Yeshua was no longer the warrior, but one who willingly laid down his life. This battle was not a

> "Not conquest, but 'salvation'—deliverance, not from human enemies only or chiefly, nor from the penalties of sin, but from the sins themselves. As spoken by the angel to the dreamer it was the answer to prayers and hopes, going beyond the hope, and purifying it from earthly thoughts."-- Charles Ellicott

physical one to be fought with swords, but a spiritual one that could only be finished one way. The Son of God had to lay down his life because only he had the power to take it up again.

"I am the good shepherd; I know my sheep and my sheep know me— just as the Father knows me and I know the Father—and I lay down my life for the sheep. I have other sheep that are not of this sheep pen. I must bring them also. They too will listen to my voice, and there shall be one flock and one shepherd. The reason my Father loves me is that I lay down my life—only to take it up again. No one takes it from me, but I lay it down of my own accord. I have authority to lay it down and authority to take it up again. This command I received from my Father."-- John 10:15-18

Notice what Jesus said about the sheep. His sheep were (and are) not exclusively the Jewish people. No, this salvation was and is available for all mankind. At this time, the Jews were waiting for political deliverance. Their concern was not for all mankind. After all, they were God's chosen people and the law required them to remain separate from Gentiles. However, God was ready to bring all people together under the name of Jesus. As the apostle Paul wrote the church in Galatia:

> So in Christ Jesus you are all children of God through faith, for all of you who were baptized into Christ have clothed yourselves with Christ. There is neither Jew nor Gentile, neither slave nor free, nor is there male and female, for you are all one in Christ Jesus. If you belong to Christ, then you are Abraham's seed, and heirs according to the promise.-- Galatians 3:26-29

Did you catch that last line? We are all Abraham's seed. That seed we've talked about with Mary. Through Christ, we become children of the promise. His victory over sin and the serpent is ours too. We become children of God when we call on the name of Jesus.

'Salvation is found in no one else, for there is no other name under heaven given to mankind by which we must be saved.' (Acts 4:12).

Salvation is available only through Jesus. Throughout history, mankind has tried to amend this fact. We've tacked on good works, we've wanted to include other religious leaders, we've figured inner peace would do something. But the Bible is clear. Jesus is the only way.

The good news here is that it doesn't rely on us in any way, shape, or form. Here's what's needed:

1. Recognize that you are a sinner.
   'If we confess our sins, he is faithful and just and will forgive us our sins and purify us from all unrighteousness.'(1 John 1:9)

2. Ask Jesus to forgive you for your sins, and acknowledge the need for his lordship.
   'If you declare with your mouth, "Jesus is Lord," and believe in your heart that God raised him from the dead, you will be saved.' (Rom 10:9)

3. Live with Jesus as a new creation!
   'I have been crucified with Christ and I no longer live, but Christ lives in me. The life I now live in the body, I live by faith in the Son of God, who loved me and gave himself for me.' (Gal 2:20)
   'Therefore, if anyone is in Christ, the new creation has come: The old has gone, the new is here!' (2 Cor 5:17)

If you've never prayed a prayer like this then I invite you to do that now. 'I tell you, now is the time of God's favor, now is the day of salvation.' (2 Cor 6:1).

Jesus came so we could live differently. Forgiveness of sins is about so much more than hell. When I was in high school there was an alternative to haunted houses called Judgement House. You started in one room where they introduced you to a family. In the next room, something catastrophic happened to the family. One year, a tornado hit a house and another year they died in a plane crash (and the gym of this church had pieces of a plane in it). Then, you saw what happened to the ones who believed in Jesus. They went to heaven where there was a dude with long hair and a bunch of little kids in white dresses and peaceful harp music. Last, you saw what happened to the ones who didn't believe. You were taken into a room that was dark and as scary as they could make it.

Actually, what came last was someone taking your group into a quiet room and giving you a pamphlet on salvation. The idea was to scare you into giving Jesus your life.

The trouble is Jesus didn't just come here to be fire insurance. Maybe some people find fear a good motivator. Perhaps it's not my place to rail against it. But I think if that's all you've ever been told then you've missed out on some of the best news.

Let me tell you about Jesus.

He's the best friend you could ever have. He's patient and good. He's faithful and kind. He defends and protects. He provides and he heals. He's with you in sorrow and hardship and suffering. He weeps with you. He loves you. In fact, he loves you so much that he moved heaven and earth to be with you. He wants you to be with him in eternity–in paradise. He's there now preparing a place for you. He's ready to intercede for you, to tell God your sins are covered and you're part of his flock. He's the Good Shepherd, who laid down his life for you and took his life up again. That's the gospel truth– 'that Christ died for our sins according to the Scriptures, that he was buried, that he was raised on the third day according to the Scriptures.' (1 Cor 15:3-4)
And if you believe that, and put your life in Jesus's hands, then all of heaven rejoices.

If you, like me, believed that a long time ago then maybe it's time to remind yourself of the good news. Sometimes the cares of this world weigh heavy. Sometimes that darkness looms so close that we think the light is in danger. But we have a hero. He has already come to save. We need only to believe.

Dear Lord Jesus, how can I ever thank you enough for coming to this dirty little planet to save me from my sins? Through you and you alone, I am saved. This Christmas I celebrate again the miracle of your birth, your death, and your resurrection. Draw me always and forever closer into a relationship with you. Make me a new creation to show your glory and goodness. In your name, I pray–Amen.

- If you've asked Jesus to be your savior, take some time to reflect on that decision. Where were you? Why did you give your life to him? How did it change your life?
- If you haven't asked Jesus to be your savior, take some time to consider why you haven't. What's holding you back? What questions do you have? What doubts or fears? Who can you talk to for answers?
- No one has all the answers, and no one has perfect faith. If you feel Jesus calling you today, then turn to him. Celebrate this Christmas as a child of God.

13) A Shepherd's Story

"And there were shepherds living out in the fields nearby,
keeping watch over their flocks at night."-- Luke 2:8

I wasn't expecting angels. Is anyone ever expecting an angel? Let alone a sky full of them? And I mean, the sky was full of angels.

But I'm getting ahead of myself.

We were living in the fields outside of Bethlehem with the sheep. It was peaceful and quiet out there. That little town was packed because of the census. Honestly, I was glad to be away from it all, under a starry sky with a few other shepherds and our flocks. Most of the time, being a shepherd isn't a job with perks. The pay is bad and folks look down on us, you know? But at least I wasn't fighting for a place to sit down in an overcrowded town.

I've wondered why the angels didn't appear in town, with all those people crowded into Bethlehem. I don't know, but maybe those people were too busy, too distracted. Maybe being a rather poor, and somewhat bored shepherd met some kind of cosmic criteria. We didn't have anywhere else to be. And when the angel appeared, he certainly had our full attention.

Let me tell you, it was terrifying. At first, anyway. Imagine a quiet, cool night with just sheep and a few friends for company. And then the appearance of a heavenly being–I can't even describe him. And the light!

The glory of the Lord lit up not just the sky, but the world around us with a light that was out of this world. To compare it even to the sun would miss the mark. Of course, we were terrified!

But somehow through all the shaking and wonder, we heard what the angel came to tell us. **"Do not be afraid! I bring you good news of great joy that will be for all the people. Today in the town of David a Savior has been born to you; he is Christ the Lord."**

A Savior? The one we've been waiting for? Of course, we weren't waiting for him out in the field that night—not like you might wait for a friend or your mother. But our people, we've been waiting for centuries, for generations. For the Savior! For all people. Poor shepherds like us. People like you too. All of us.

Our terror turned to joy in the blink of a tearful eye. I couldn't help crying with joy—and wonder and awe. The angel told us where to find this baby—wrapped in swaddling cloths and lying in a manger. When he finished speaking, the entire sky filled with angels. An entire company of angels broke through to tell us the news. And we didn't miss the message!

And we didn't waste any time either. We ran into Bethlehem, looking everywhere for this baby lying in a manger. We found him with his parents. Joseph was just an ordinary carpenter, not much different than me. Mary was wide-eyed with wonder just like us when we told her our story and soaked up every word to hold in her heart. I know I'll never forget it either.

We told everyone we saw what had happened. We couldn't stop glorifying and praising God for everything we had heard and seen that night. People were amazed when they heard our story. I'm still amazed myself! I wasn't expecting an angel. I wasn't expecting anyone to come tell me when the Messiah was born—but I'm glad I didn't miss it.

- What if the shepherds had ignored the message? What if they had started to find the stable, and then got distracted by the sheep, or the weather, or something else less important? Would it have mattered to them? Would it matter to us to not have their visit recorded?
- Would you have responded the same way the shepherds did? Or would you have stopped to ask questions?

14) That's What Christmas Is All About

But the angel said to them, "Do not be afraid. I bring you good news that will cause great joy for all the people.-- Luke 2:10

★**Read Luke 2:8-20**

Anyone who has seen *A Charlie Brown Christmas* has heard today's scripture reading. Charles Schulz had to fight CBS for the famous scene of Linus reciting the Bible to be included. CBS felt it was too religious for a cartoon. It was too controversial for television. Schulz adamantly replied to producer Bill Mendelson, "Bill, if we don't do it, who will? We can do it...Look, if we're going to do this, we should talk about what Christmas is all about, not just do a cartoon with no particular point of view." [3]In the end, Schulz was proved right. The Christmas special went on to win a Primetime Emmy for Outstanding Children's Program, and it aired on television every year from 1965 until 2022 when it moved to a streaming platform.

It's a powerful scene, isn't it? Charlie Brown has been worrying about everything. His dog, his sister, the play, the tree, Lucy, and mostly himself. I get it. The holidays tend to do that to me too. Distractions galore and the pressure to get things right is crushing. If you're already a little on the neurotic side like Charlie Brown and me, the Christmas season can really do a number on you.

---

[3] Foust, Michael. "How Charles Schulz Fought for Jesus In *Charlie Brown Christmas*" ChristianHeadlines.Com, ChristianHeadlines.com, 24 Dec. 2019, www.christianheadlines.com/contributors/michael-foust/how-charles-schulz-fought-for-jesus-in-a-charlie-brown-christmas.html#google_vignette

Then, Linus interrupts with this startling moment of clarity. Notice how all the chaos comes to a halt in this quiet moment. Just a kid on a stage with a spotlight. He even sets his blanket down so he can gesture at the most important moment in the story. "And that's what Christmas is all about, Charlie Brown."

Charles Schulz cut through the Christmas cacophony with this passage—the shepherds watching their flocks by night and angels singing Gloria. I think he was onto something. Let's lean into this one and see what we discover.

Per usual, the shepherds' first reaction to the angels was that of terror. Now, this one I can really understand. They were prepared for danger---a lion or some other animal that would like a tasty sheep for a midnight snack--but they were not prepared for angels. Who would be? And this time, not just one. Not just Gabriel. This time he brought his friends. Scripture tells us it was 'a great company of the heavenly host.' A company is a military term. This is part of God's Angel Army reporting for duty, but with swords sheathed. They're not here to battle, but to proclaim, to rejoice. They come with words of peace and goodwill.

Imagine how incredible it would be to see the dark night sky lit up with the glow of a company of angels in God's army. Imagine the sound of them singing. What a moment this must have been.

The angels returned to heaven after making their announcement and praising God, then the shepherds had to figure out what to do next. I sorta imagine that the first thing they did was to pick each other up off the ground due to shock. And then, they went to find the baby.

Here's the thing to remember: we're used to hearing this story. We know that Jesus was born in a stable and his first bed was a manger. It seems normal to us because this story has been told for over two thousand years now. But when it happened, it wasn't normal

Think back to a time when you heard the news of a birth. I remember when my first niece was born–on my husband's birthday no less! She was born in a hospital, swaddled up safe and warm, and put in one of those hospital bassinets. She wasn't born in a barn and put in a feeding trough. That's just not a thing we do. And it wasn't what was normal then either. But it's exactly what happened with Mary, Joseph, and Jesus. And it's what the shepherds were told to go find.

The shepherds found the baby because they were looking for something so out of the ordinary. Maybe other babies were born in Bethlehem that night--who knows? But only one was born in a stable and lying in a manger. Do you think maybe the shepherds weren't convinced they were going to find the baby? That it wouldn't be just as the angels told them? But it was exactly as the angels said. We can trust God's message to us.

I wonder what Mary and Joseph thought when these shepherds found them. Think back to when John the Baptist was born. Remember how births were celebrated by all the relatives and neighbors with singing and feasting? But because of the census Jesus was born far from their home in Galilee, and as far as we know, there was no one there with them. No one to celebrate.

Until God provided the celebrants. Do you really think he would let his own son come into the world without some rejoicing? Puh-lease.

Sure, he was born in a stable and not a palace. The elite didn't fawn over him. Jesus didn't need that kind of prestige. Shepherds will do. And they did. They came, they saw, and they rejoiced. I bet this did much to comfort Mary and Joseph. What a God-wink, right?

Do you wonder why shepherds? Maybe Mary and Joseph looked at each other after the shepherds departed and asked that very question. Not out of ingratitude, mind you, but sheer curiosity. Of all the people in Bethlehem and Judea, shepherds?

They weren't exactly the upper crust of society. Uneducated and probably scruffy dirty (as my aunt might say). Arguably no one's first choice— except God.

It's true that Jesus came for all people, the poor as well as the rich. Every strata of society needs his gift of grace. Everyone. But there's more here. Another layer that only God would weave into his story.

First, Jesus describes himself as the Good Shepherd. We are his flock and he has come to gather us under his protection. He is a fierce defender, willing to lay down his life–and able to take it up again.

Second, Bethlehem shepherds tended the flocks for the temple. The law required two unblemished one-year-old lambs to be sacrificed every day, one in the morning and one at twilight. Let that sink in. That's over seven hundred lambs a year, and that's only for daily sacrifice. There were many occasions which required additional sacrifices. Curiously enough, just today in my daily study I read the passage in Exodus where God outlines all of this for Moses for the first time. I didn't expect that it would be connected to the Christmas story. But it does. Of course, it does.

The wages of sin is death. After reading Exodus 29, I wrote in my Bible: *so much blood and sacrifice was required*. For sin. And it was over and over and over and over again. Every day. Every morning, every twilight. Every year on high holy days.

Until Jesus. The perfect sacrifice. The truly unblemished lamb of God. Remember that's what John the Baptist called him. Every element of the Christmas story points us to the cross. It's not only about a baby swaddled in a manger but the lamb of God who takes away the sins of the world. So, of course, shepherds. *These* shepherds. The ones who tended the flocks for the temple sacrifice. These men protected these sheep and watched over them faithfully through all the watches of the night. And they were the first ones to behold the lamb of God.

It's beautiful, isn't it? This careworn quilt we've draped over us for years has more love and intention in its threads than we realized. This patch here made of lamb's wool is what Christmas is all about.

Heavenly Father, you've always known exactly what you were doing, even if it doesn't make sense to me. Each detail of the Christmas story shows us your provision and grace. You provided celebrants, both angelic and lowly, to rejoice in the birth of your son. And your son was the most important provision of all. Sending him to be the perfect lamb, to bear my sins, and be the sacrifice that could finally make things right. What a night this must have been for you, for the shepherds, for Mary and Joseph. What a night it is for me to remember and to thank you. Always I thank you—Amen.

- Back to Charlie Brown for a moment. Do you remember what part Linus is assigned in their play? A shepherd. Watch the special with new eyes this year and ask yourself who you can share this simple message with—it's far more than a cartoon.
- The shepherds didn't require anything for their trip except directions. Upon arrival, they didn't feel anything but welcomed. Who can you welcome into your celebration this year? Is there someone you know who can't bring anything except themselves but who may, in fact, be a big part of your celebration?

15) The Rest of the Story

When they had seen him, they spread the word concerning
what had been told them about this child, and all who heard it were amazed
at what the shepherds said to them.-- Luke 2:17-18

But wait–there's more! Call now...

Just kidding. This isn't an infomercial. But there is more to the shepherd's story. I just couldn't pack it all into one day. As my pastor says, why do it in one message when you can do it in two?

What did the shepherds do after they saw Jesus? They told everyone about him! The people were astonished by their story. They wondered and marveled, but as far as we know, no one came to investigate. No one went looking for themselves for this babe swaddled in a manger.

I have a massive collection of Christmas picture books–a couple hundred. There's one about the birth of Jesus, and the entire town comes out to dance around the

"The shepherds were plain, downright, honest men, and they could not suspect them guilty of any design to impose upon them; what they had said therefore was likely to be true, and, if true, they could not but wonder at it, that the Messiah should be born in a stable and not in a palace, that angels should bring news of it to poor shepherds and not to the chief priests. They wondered, but never enquired any further about the Saviour, their duty to him, or advantages by him, but let the thing drop as a nine days' wonder. O the amazing stupidity of the men of that generation! Justly were the things which belonged to their peace hid from their eyes, when they thus wilfully shut their eyes against them."-- Matthew Henry stable. It's a lovely book with a beautiful sentiment. But it just isn't true. The people didn't come. They didn't get out of their beds to come see. They didn't dance. Maybe that's why most of the religious Christmas books I have are about animals recognizing Jesus as a remarkable baby. I'm not here to tell you that they did–that the animals talked at midnight and all that folklore. But I can see why writers for children's books often end up in that camp. Facts are facts and the people didn't come, even after the shepherds told them the good news.

Does this mean the shepherds shouldn't have bothered? Should they have just talked about it amongst themselves? If the people wanted to know, they knew where to find them.

Um, no. The shepherds became the first evangelists. And just because the people didn't respond with much more than wide eyes (and probably the rumor mill started) doesn't mean they wasted their time. The fact is, we don't know how God used the seeds they planted.

We need to tell people about Jesus, too. People may be astonished by our stories--some might not believe us. It might sound too good to be true, or just too unbelievable. But some will find the hope and joy they've been looking for all their lives.

Stay with me here. This material was first written as a set of Advent lessons for children. It looked much different then. Much. But I didn't grow up in a liturgical tradition, and I wanted to write some lessons that introduced it as well as a thorough walk through the Christmas story.

Each candle in Advent has a name and a theme. The first week is the Prophet's Candle (or sometimes Mary's Candle), and the theme is hope.

The second week is The Bethlehem Candle, and the theme is faith. The third candle is The Shepherd's Candle and the theme is joy. The fourth candle is the Angel's Candle and the theme is peace. And the fifth candle, the white one, is the Christ candle and the theme is love. (Side note: there is some variance to the themes depending on denomination or particular traditions).

Originally, Advent was a season more like Lent. It was a quiet time when the harvest was over and the nights were longer for contemplation. People often fasted as they prepared for the big feast on Christ's Mass. On the third week of Advent, Gaudette Sunday, the Shepherd's Candle was lit and there was a break from fasting. This is why sometimes the third candle is pink instead of purple–pink symbolizes joy. This week was different from the others. It was a time of great joy.

I want you to notice the last thing Luke tells us about the shepherds.

'The shepherds returned, glorifying and praising God for all the things they had heard and seen, which were just as they had been told.'-- Luke 2:20

The shepherds also returned to their fields. After all, they are shepherds. That's what they do. But what else did they do? They glorified and praised God. They returned to their ordinary lives but with extraordinary joy. Worship isn't only for church or somewhere special. It's for every day. The shepherds went about their business, as they were doing before the angels appeared, but now they were glorifying and praising God.

I'm going to close today with the original words I wrote for those Advent lessons. I think it works for grown-ups too.

Why does Jesus' birth give us joy? Why were the angels singing praises, and the shepherds glorifying God? Jesus is the savior for the entire world. Every person who has ever lived anywhere at any time on planet Earth needs Jesus. We are lost in sin without him.

God always had a plan to save us. But there was a long, long time between Adam and Eve eating the fruit in the garden, and Jesus being born in Bethlehem. Thousands of years, in fact.

Because of Jesus, we can be restored to God. We can be friends with him again when we ask Jesus for forgiveness of our sins, thank him for paying the price of our sins on the cross, and trust him to be the leader of our lives. The curse of sin is broken! This is why there is always a reason to be joyful.

Who knows the song "Joy to the World"? Did you know that song isn't about Jesus being born? We sing it at Christmastime, but it is actually about Jesus coming again.

Jesus will come again. He won't come as a baby but as a grown-up. When he comes again, it will be as a king to set up his kingdom forever and ever. The Bible talks about this a lot in the book of Revelation. Some of it is scary--because Jesus will have to get rid of all the evil in the earth. But we don't need to be afraid. When Jesus comes, he will make the earth perfect again. All things will be made new. And we will never feel lonely, scared, or sad again.

The people waited for a long time for the Messiah to come, and many of them missed it. Sometimes you can wait so long for something, you might stop believing it's going to happen. Christians have been waiting for two thousand years for Jesus to come back. Some people have stopped believing it will ever happen. But the Bible tells us to be ready.

What does it mean to be ready? Here are a few examples: To have that relationship with Jesus as your savior, to trust and obey him, and to tell others about him.

As we get ready for Christmas this year, let's also look forward to Jesus coming again. It will be the biggest and best celebration--far better than anything we could ever imagine!

Dear Lord Jesus, I'm waiting for you to come again as you said you would. Help me to wait expectantly and not stop believing in your promised return. Give me the words to share your story with people who need to hear it. In your name—Amen.

- Is it easy or hard for you to tell people about Jesus? Do you feel uncomfortable? Worried you might offend someone? Come on too strong? I get it—me too. Pray for the right opportunities to unfold with the people God brings into your life. Remember, it's not your job to save souls, but it is your joy to tell someone what Jesus means to you.
- How can you bring more rejoicing and praising God into your everyday life?

16) Gabriel's Story

The angel said to him, "I am Gabriel. I stand in the presence of God, and I have been sent to speak to you and to tell you this good news.-- Luke 1:19

We always knew there was a plan. After Lucifer's rebellion, after the fall in Eden, after Noah, and Abraham, and Moses, and David, and all the law and prophets. In the fullness of time, He would send his son to make things right again. At last, the time had come–the plan was starting to unfold, and there was gloriously good news to tell. I was honored to be the one the Lord chose as his messenger. Each time the Lord summoned me, I went straight away to deliver the good news. When God sends you on assignment, you don't delay.

Zechariah, the old childless priest, surprised me. For years, he and his wife Elizabeth had prayed for a child. Now God was giving them a son! Not only that but their son would grow up to prepare the way for the Messiah. I was expecting joy, excitement, tears of relief and happiness. But Zechariah only asked me how he could be sure it was true. Imagine, doubting an angel of the Lord! Doubting God himself! Maybe humans have a hard time believing when they've been waiting a long time. But after months of silence, Zechariah held his son John–and praised God. Now he knows God's plans and promises are true.

Then there was Mary. This young woman who never asked for anything special, never expected God's favor, was chosen to be the mother of the Son of God. She wondered how this would be–not if it could be. I told her **"Nothing is impossible with God."** And she replied simply, **"Let it be as you have said"**. Though she never could have expected this, Mary said yes to God's plan.

So did Joseph, The carpenter with calloused hands and a godly heart. He didn't want to disgrace Mary, now with child before their marriage. In a dream, I told him to marry her, to trust God, and to name the baby Jesus because he will save his people from their sins. When Joseph woke from this dream, he obeyed. Despite the glares, stares, and whispers, he trusted God's plan.

When Jesus, at last, was born I was bursting to announce the good news. I waited in excited anticipation to see where God would send me with this message of great joy. Perhaps a priest again. Or maybe this time a king.

But on this sacred, glorious night God sent me to shepherds. It seemed a curious choice. Even so, without delay–I appeared in a field outside Bethlehem to a handful of terrified shepherds. I couldn't wait to turn their fear into joy. **"Do not be afraid! I bring you good news of great joy that will be for all the people! Today in the town of David, a Savior has been born to you; he is Christ the Lord! This will be a sign to you: You will find a baby wrapped in cloths and lying in a manger."**

At that moment, the entire heavenly host joined me. How could any angel resist praising God at such a moment as this? The countryside and all of heaven echoed with praise: **"Glory to God in the highest, and on earth peace, goodwill to men!"**

The shepherds ran to find him. And I understood why God had chosen these ordinary shepherds. They didn't waste a moment. They didn't stop to debate if our message could be true, or how strange it was to look for a baby in a manger. They didn't pause for a bite to eat or to change into their best clothes. They ran for Bethlehem and didn't stop until they found the baby. And after seeing Jesus, the shepherds told everyone what had happened and what I had said about this child. All who heard their story were astonished.

God's plan was finally being revealed. Jesus had entered the world to save mankind from their sins! To restore what had been lost in the fall, to take back what Lucifer had taken captive. We always knew there was a plan. And no plan of God will ever fail.

- Think about a time when you were truly joyous. What were the circumstances? Did others share your joy?
- The angels' message was for mankind, not for themselves. Do you ever get excited about the good news that others receive?
- Imagine for a moment what it was like for them to return to heaven having completed their task.

17) Son and Savior

Today in the town of David a Savior has been born to you;
he is the Messiah, the Lord.-- Luke 2:11

I'm not giving you a specific scripture passage to look up today. We're going to be moving through a few passages, and I've decided to include them here for you. We're going to chart Gabriel's course through the Bible.

It turns out that the very first time Gabriel makes a named appearance is in the book of Daniel. Many people are familiar with the first few chapters of Daniel where we meet Shadrach, Meschach, Abednego, and Daniel himself. They are exiled as captives in Babylon and forced to serve under multiple kings as their time there unfolds.

Then, in chapter eight Daniel recorded an apocalyptic vision that "appalled" him. And this is where we first meet Gabriel. He was sent to explain the vision to Daniel. I'm not going to even attempt that here and now as that's a rabbit we don't need to chase today. It suffices enough to say that Daniel shared "I, Daniel, was exhausted and lay ill for several days....I was appalled by the vision; it was beyond understanding."

In the next chapter, we read that Daniel pleaded with God to forgive Israel and bring them back to Jerusalem. It's an earnest prayer, heartfelt and sorrowful. And Gabriel was sent to him again.

> While I was speaking and praying, confessing my sin and the sin of
> my people Israel and making my request to the Lord my God for
> his holy hill—while I was still in prayer, Gabriel, the man I had seen
> in the earlier vision, came to me in swift flight about the time of the

evening sacrifice. He instructed me and said to me, "Daniel, I have now come to give you insight and understanding. As soon as you began to pray, a word went out, which I have come to tell you, for you are highly esteemed. Therefore, consider the word and understand the vision: – Daniel 9:20-23

I share this because it confirms to us that God is actively listening to our prayers. At the moment Daniel began to pray, a word was sent. A word already prepared and destined for Daniel. In Matthew 6:8 Jesus said, "...your Father knows you need before you ask him." Daniel needed explanations and assurances, and Gabriel was prepared to give him both.

What happens next is an explanation about end times and the 'Anointed One'. This is the first recorded revelation of Jesus from the mouth of Gabriel–about five hundred years before he appeared to Zechariah. The rest of his message here in Daniel is quite interesting, at least among scholars and theologians who like to debate things like 'are numbers in the Bible symbolic or literal' and 'what is the proper way to count years'. As tempting as it is for me to chase this particular rabbit, I'm going to resist it. You're welcome (unless you're into that, in which case, I'm sorry).

> "It would appear that as God has set in order the things of the universe, that He probably placed Gabriel as the overseer in charge of the details of getting His Son into the world. Preparing the people on the earth, preparing Mary, because it was Gabriel who appeared to Mary. Preparing here Zacharias. It would seem that he has a hard time keeping secrets. He appeared five hundred years earlier and spilled the beans to Daniel of a time that the Messiah would be coming. And so here he is again, some five hundred years later."-- Chuck Smith

But there are a few rabbits we are going to chase. Specifically, we're going to look at the words of Gabriel and see what he revealed about the nature and character of Jesus. I've put specific words in **bold** for emphasis.

To Daniel in answer to prayer:
"Know and understand this: From the time the word goes out to restore and rebuild Jerusalem until the **Anointed One,** the ruler, comes, there will be seven 'sevens,' and sixty-two 'sevens.' It will be rebuilt with streets and a trench, but in times of trouble. After the sixty-two 'sevens,' the **Anointed One** will be put to death and will have nothing. The people of the ruler who will come will destroy the city and the sanctuary. The end will come like a flood: War will continue until the end, and desolations have been decreed. " –Daniel 9:25-26

- The Hebrew word 'Messiah' and the Greek word 'Christ' both mean 'Anointed One'. Kings and priests were anointed, and Jesus is both the King of Kings and our High Priest. Additionally, the people anticipated the Messiah as their savior.

To Zechariah regarding the birth of his son, John the Baptist
"And he will go on before **the Lord,** in the spirit and power of Elijah, to turn the hearts of the parents to their children and the disobedient to the wisdom of the righteous—to make ready a people prepared for **the Lord.**"-- Luke 1:17

- We understand that when Gabriel says 'the Lord' he is speaking of Jesus. The word for 'Lord' here is the Greek word 'kyrios' which means 'supreme in authority'.

To Mary
"You will conceive and give birth to a son, and you are to call him **Jesus**. He will be great and will be called the **Son of the Most High**. The Lord God will give him the throne of his father David, and he will reign over Jacob's

descendants forever; his kingdom will never end. The Holy Spirit will come on you, and the power of the Most High will overshadow you. So the holy one to be born will be called the **Son of God**."-- Luke 1:31-33, 35

To Joseph
"She will give birth to a son, and you are to give him the name **Jesus, because he will save his people from their sins**".-- Matthew 1:21

To the Shepherds
"Do not be afraid. I bring you good news that will cause great joy for all the people. Today in the town of David a **Savior** has been born to you; he is the **Messiah, the Lord**".--Luke 2:10-11

Over and over again, Gabriel speaks of the unique role of Jesus. Every name he used pointed to two things: 1) Jesus is the Son of the Most High God, and 2) he is the Savior. There is such profound hope here. When Daniel despaired in prayer, Gabriel told him about Jesus. And we can preach the gospel to ourselves when the weight of sin and brokenness feels heavy on our shoulders. Jesus came so that we don't have to carry that weight on our own. I think when Gabriel came to Daniel it was to assure him that there was still hope for Jerusalem–a Savior was coming. And, my friends, he is coming again.

Father God, thank you for hearing my prayers and knowing what I need even before I ask. Help me hold onto the hope I have in Jesus–your one and only son, and my savior. Amen

- How does the coming of Jesus give you hope? How about the second coming?
- What does it mean to preach the gospel to yourself?

18) The Song of Salvation

"Glory to God in the highest heaven,
and on earth peace to those on whom his favor rests."-- Luke 2:14

If you're anything like me, anytime you read the verse at the top of this page in anything other than the KJV your brain twitches a little. I'm going back to *A Charlie Brown Christmas* to place blame on Linus Van Pelt. He recited it to us like this: "Glory to God in the highest, and on earth peace, goodwill toward men." And it just *sounds* good, right? I mean, it flows. It sounds like music. The other translation feels a little clunky, at least, for singing.

But apparently, it is the more accurate translation. However, I'm getting ahead of myself. Let's wrap ourselves up in the angel's song of praise for a while and see what comforts are there for us.

Their song began with 'Glory to God in the highest.' God is the object of their praise. Glory belongs to God, and God alone. This is the crux of the matter. Lucifer envied God's glory and desired to have it for himself. This caused him and a third of the angels who took his side to be cast out of heaven. Outraged and now the embodiment of evil, Lucifer sought to destroy God's most beloved creation: man. Humans, created in the likeness of God, became his most favorite target. Adam and Eve took the bait: they desired to be like God. And the chaos that has followed can be felt in every broken heart in every human breast ever since.

Glory can only belong to God. I wrote this sentence and then asked myself: Why? What exactly *is* glory? It feels like one of those church-words we toss around with a general understanding of what we mean. So I looked it up, and in Luke 2:14 it comes from the Greek word 'doxa' and it means 'dignity, honor, praise, worship.' Doxa...like 'The Doxology' which we sang every single Sunday in my Grammy and PapPap's church when I was a kid.

'Praise God from whom all blessings flow. Praise him, ye creatures here below. Praise him, above ye heavenly hosts. Praise Father, Son, and Holy Ghost. Amen.'

Ha, I did that from memory. Nothing like music to leave a good mark on the gray matter. But this is helpful. Glory is honor and praise and worship. It also speaks to splendor and brightness. To majesty and authority. I can see why Lucifer wanted it for himself. And I can see how we humans wear ourselves out chasing it. Don't think you do?

How much does it bother you when you post something on social media and get exactly zero likes or comments? How about when you work really hard on something and no one so much as notices it or gives you any thanks? What about if you do the work, and someone else gets credit? Kinda gets to you, doesn't it? I'll be honest: it drives me crazy. I thrive on recognition and validation, and I don't get nearly enough of it to really satisfy me.

Because I don't think there's enough that ever could. We always want a little more. Like John D. Rockefeller, the infamous millionaire, said when asked how much was enough money– "just a little bit more". It wasn't enough for Lucifer to be a bright and beautiful angel (Ezekiel 28), he desired more. And it wasn't enough for Adam and Eve to have access to every tree in the Garden, save the Tree of Knowledge of Good and Evil. They desired that one too. Just a little bit more.

This is the need for the Incarnation in the first place. To fix what has been broken ever since that fateful bite of fruit in the Garden of Eden.

This leads me to the next part: "and on earth peace..." At that moment in history when the angels sang these words, Jews were under Roman oppression. The reality of the shepherds was that of intense taxation, few legal rights, and the lingering threat of Roman brutality. This era under Caesar Augustus has been nicknamed the 'Pax Romana' but it was only good times and plenty for the Romans. Deliverance from this oppression is what the Jewish people were craving. Yet it wasn't the reason for the angels' song. They sang of something far more sacred and more needed. The song of salvation. Consider this quote from Charles Spurgeon, who was far more eloquent than me:

> Wars had raged from the ends of the world; men had slaughtered one another, heaps on heaps. There had been wars within as well as wars without. Conscience had fought with man; Satan had tormented man with thoughts of sin. There had been no peace on earth since Adam fell. But, now, when the newborn King made his appearance, the swaddling band with which he was wrapped up was the white flag of peace. That manger was the place where the treaty was signed, whereby warfare should be stopped between man's conscience and himself, man's conscience and his God... Do you not feel my brethren, that the gospel of God is peace to man? Where else can peace be found, but in the message of Jesus?.. And what a peace it is, beloved! It is peace like a river, and righteousness like the waves of the sea. It is the peace of God that passeth all understanding, which keeps our hearts and minds through Jesus Christ our Lord. This sacred peace between the pardoned soul and God the pardoner; this marvelous at-one-ment between the sinner

and his judge, this was it that the angels sung when they said, "peace on earth."

And now we're back where I started–that awkward translation bit. But I think we can begin to understand the angels' song now, whichever way we prefer to read it in English. The goodwill toward men is specific. It's not just warm fuzzies from God beamed to Earth like he's a proud papa handing out cigars to every guy in the waiting room. God's goodwill is extended to 'those on whom his favor rests'. And who is that?

The ones who believe in his son. Those who call upon the name of Jesus to be saved. The redeemed.

We're captives in this war between Good and Evil, Dark and Light, Sin and Holiness. And captives must be ransomed by their King. That's how it works. I went through a phase a few years ago where I binge-watched a movie version of William Shakespeare's *Henry the Fifth* over and over again. In this play, King Henry is baited by France into war. There's a particular parcel of France which English kings time and again laid claim to, and it's to this area that Henry goes to show his dominance to the French king. Things don't go too well for Henry for a while. His men are dying, not just in battle but from sickness and exhaustion too. He dresses in disguise one night and walks among the men. Then, he overhears some of them debating whether or not he would ransom them if they were taken captive. And all I could think about was Jesus.

We're so far removed from this kind of world. The language seems reserved for the Bible and Shakespeare and the distant past. I've grown up with words like 'redemption' and 'ransom' connected to salvation but never saw it in living color like this.

The men in that play worried that their king wouldn't bother to ransom them. They figured their lives weren't worth what it would cost him. They were nothing but foot soldiers—nameless and nothing to a king concerned with his own glory and kingdom. Throughout history, we have seen kings like that. Even now, I'd argue there are rulers and politicians who care only for themselves and not the people they're meant to represent and protect.

Jesus is not that kind of king. He's not that kind of ruler. We're worth so much to him that he ransomed us with his *own life*. His blood was poured out for us. His body was broken for us.

And that's why the angels were singing that night in Bethlehem. The whole cosmic story came to a point here first. A child was born—the Word became flesh and dwelled among us. A son was given—the Son of Man came to give his life as a ransom for many (Matthew 20:28).

God, I join the angel chorus today in praising you. Glory belongs to you and you alone. I seek it for myself sometimes, Lord, and I repent today. Give me instead your peace; the peace that comes from knowing you bought me at a price and I am no longer a captive of sin and fear. Thank you for your peace and goodwill toward me. It's beautiful, no matter how I say it. Amen.

- Reflect today on ways you seek your own glory. How can you reorient yourself to giving glory to God?
- Does the illustration from *Henry the Fifth* give you a clearer picture of what it means to be ransomed? What kind of king is Jesus? What kind of assurance do we have with him as our king?

19) Anna's Story

Coming up to them at that very moment, she gave thanks to God and spoke about the child to all who were looking forward to the redemption of Jerusalem.-- Luke 2:38

For most of my life, I made the temple my home. Like the sparrows in the psalm[4], I found a home near the altar of the Lord. I stayed at the temple fasting and praying, worshiping night and day.

Admittedly, it's not what other widows would do. My husband died after only seven years together. I've often thought of this on a quiet evening alone. Seven means completeness, wholeness. I suppose we had a whole marriage then, in just those seven years.

So, I gave the rest of my life to worship the Lord in his courts. I've been there every morning to see the smoke rise when the lamb is offered, and again in the evening. I've smelled the incense as it wafts heavenward. Though I've never entered the Holy Place, I've offered my prayers as faithfully as the priests. Prayers for our people. Prayers for the redemption of Jerusalem. Like the prophets of old, I've longed to see God's mighty arm move and redeem his people. To make his name renowned in all the earth.

And then he came. Fussing and small and the joy of his parents. I knew him in an instant. The Spirit made him known to me. That wee little baby they brought to the temple for dedication–he was the hope of Israel.

To be sure, they were poor. The law requires a year-old lamb, or if that is

---

[4] Psalm 84:3

too costly, a pair of doves or pigeons. Mary offered this second option. They were poor but faithful. They did everything just as it is written, and with earnest hearts too. When you spend as much time around the temple as I have you get a sense for things. I've witnessed the puffed-up prayers and offerings of the proud, and the humble and honest offerings of the meek.

I wasn't the only one who noticed them that day. Simeon was also at the temple. Righteous and devout—never puffed up or proud—he was waiting for the consolation of Israel. Like me, Simeon's hope was in the Lord. We often saw each other over the many years we each spent praying and worshiping at the temple. And when Simeon saw that baby, he knew just as surely as I did.

In fact—Simeon saw him first. **Moved by the Spirit, he went into the temple courts. When the parents brought in the child Jesus to do for him what the custom of the Law required, Simeon took him in his arms and praised God, saying:**

"Sovereign Lord, as you have promised,
    you may now dismiss your servant in peace.
For my eyes have seen your salvation,
    which you have prepared in the sight of all nations:
a light for revelation to the Gentiles,
    and the glory of your people Israel."

The child's father and mother marveled at what was said about him. Then Simeon blessed them and said to Mary, his mother: "This child is destined to cause the falling and rising of many in Israel, and to be a sign that will be spoken against, so that the thoughts of many hearts will be revealed. And a sword will pierce your own soul too."

And it was at this very moment that I saw them. Quickly, I joined Simeon in thanking God for this baby. I approached this young couple, my heart swelling. Tears welled in my eyes and a laugh bubbled in my chest. The joy of the Lord has been my strength all these many years. At last, to behold him–the Anointed One! I started telling everyone about Jesus that day–and I haven't stopped.

That's why I'm telling you about him today. This little baby is going to grow up to be the redemption of Jerusalem. He will grow **like a tender shoot, and like a root out of dry ground. A shoot will come up from the stump of Jesse; from his roots a Branch will bear fruit. The Spirit of the Lord will rest on him—**

    the Spirit of wisdom and of understanding,

    the Spirit of counsel and of might,

    the Spirit of the knowledge and fear of the Lord—

and he will delight in the fear of the Lord.[5]

In that day the Root of Jesse will stand as a banner for the peoples; the nations will rally to him, and his resting place will be glorious.

  He will raise a banner for the nations

    and gather the exiles of Israel;

he will assemble the scattered people of Judah

    from the four quarters of the earth.[6]

All your children will be taught by the Lord,

    and great will be their peace.[7] [8]

---

[5] Isaiah 11:1-3

[6] Isaiah 11:1-3, 10, 12

[7] Isaiah 54:13

[8] Note from Rebecca: Nothing in the text of Luke 2 indicates Anna quoted the prophet Isaiah. However, Luke describes her as a prophetess and he says she 'spoke about the child to all who were looking forward to the redemption of Israel' so I felt that it fit her well.

- Anna and Simeon were both waiting to see the Messiah. They were waiting with the expectation of seeing him in their lifetime. How do you think that changed how they lived? How they worshipped? How they spoke to others?
- How do you think encountering Jesus, even as an infant, changed them?
- Anna was unafraid to join Simeon as he spoke to Mary and Joseph. She didn't watch from afar. Like the shepherds, she went toward the Christ child. And then she told everyone she encountered about him. How can you follow her example?

20) Two Witnesses

"For my eyes have seen your salvation, which you have prepared in the sight of
all nations: a light for revelation to the Gentiles,
and the glory of your people Israel."-- Luke 2:30-32

★ **Read Luke 2:21-40**

Most of the time we get to the cozy little scene in the stable, sing a few
choruses of 'Come Let us Adore Him', and call it a day. That's the
Christmas story, right? Right.

But we're going to extend our study a little further. For one reason, it's
simply practical for me. Those first Advent lessons I wrote for kids started
with week one of Advent but ended with The Epiphany in January. I
needed a lesson to fill in that one week between the end of Advent and the
Epiphany. Enter Simeon and Anna.

Plus, if we read the Bible chronologically, weaving the accounts of
Matthew and Luke together, then Jesus's presentation at the temple is the
next event in the timeline. But why? Let's look at a couple of verses from
the Old Testament for some context.

The Lord said to Moses, "Consecrate to me every firstborn male.
The first offspring of every womb among the Israelites belongs to
me, whether human or animal."-- Exodus 13:2

The Lord said to Moses, "Say to the Israelites: 'A woman who
becomes pregnant and gives birth to a son will be ceremonially

unclean for seven days, just as she is unclean during her monthly period. On the eighth day the boy is to be circumcised. Then the woman must wait thirty-three days to be purified from her bleeding. She must not touch anything sacred or go to the sanctuary until the days of her purification are over... When the days of her purification for a son or daughter are over, she is to bring to the priest at the entrance to the tent of meeting a year-old lamb for a burnt offering and a young pigeon or a dove for a sin offering. He shall offer them before the Lord to make atonement for her, and then she will be ceremonially clean from her flow of blood...But if she cannot afford a lamb, she is to bring two doves or two young pigeons, one for a burnt offering and the other for a sin offering. In this way the priest will make atonement for her, and she will be clean.'"-- Leviticus 12:1-4, 6-8

As we read through Luke 2, we see Mary and Joseph following the law exactly as prescribed. In verse 21, Luke reported that they took Jesus for circumcision when he was eight days old. During the rites of circumcision, he was officially given the name Jesus, 'the name the angel had given him before he was conceived.' (Luke 2:21)

Then, when Jesus was forty days old, he was presented at the temple when Mary went for the purification ceremony. She offered a pair of doves or two young pigeons. This was the option for people who could not afford to offer a year-old lamb for sacrifice. Therefore, this must have taken place *before* the Magi came and gave Jesus valuable gifts. Modern nativity scenes show the Magi at the stable. But the Biblical text simply doesn't support this. We'll get into that more soon. Everything so far seems to have been pretty ordinary. Mary and Joseph seemed like any other couple with their firstborn son.

Until Simeon entered the scene, moved by the Holy Spirit. Like John the Baptist leaping in his mother's womb, Elizabeth blessing Mary, Zechariah praising and prophesying. The Holy Spirit was very active throughout the Christmas story.

The Spirit prompted Simeon to enter the temple courts where he would find Mary, Joseph, and Jesus. I appreciate that Luke took a minute to introduce folks to us as they enter the narrative. Of Simeon, he wrote: "Now there was a man in Jerusalem called Simeon, who was righteous and devout. He was waiting for the consolation of Israel, and the Holy Spirit was on him. It had been revealed to him by the Holy Spirit that he would not die before he had seen the Lord's Messiah."(2:25-26)

Some scholars believe Simeon was a priest as it would explain why he was in the temple vicinity, and why Mary so willingly let him take Jesus into his arms. Still, it's neither here nor there really if he was a priest or not. He was a righteous man who was living expectantly for the Messiah. And he wasn't so caught up in his own ideas of what that Messiah was supposed to look like that he missed it. Simeon was eager to receive this wee baby when many people overlooked him waiting for a warrior.

Imagine this old man, his eyes filled with wonder and joy as he peers at the little one in his arms. His thoughts swim not with memories of his own sweet babies as he might with any other baby, but with the mercies of God. Peace washes over him. The wait is over. He can enter God's rest. He has seen the Savior.

Time and again throughout his ministry people demanded Jesus give them signs to prove he was the Son of God. They could not believe in him without seeing a demonstration of power. But what kind of demonstration could this baby have given Simeon? None. None at all.

I took a World Literature course in college. In it, I learned that in the Quran's version of the birth of Jesus, he talks. As a newborn! In fact, some of the apocryphal gospels written in the second century have similar stories of Baby Jesus talking or doing miracles. Yet, Luke wrote no such report. Neither did Matthew, or Mark, or John. For all intents and purposes, Jesus acted just exactly like a regular baby.

Simeon didn't need a sign from the Savior to believe. He had all the confirmation he needed for the Spirit to trust that this baby would grow into the 'a light for revelation to the Gentiles, and the glory of your people Israel.' (Luke 2:32)

Who are the Gentiles? Anyone who isn't a Jew. The Jews are God's chosen people, going all the way back to Abraham in the book of Genesis. God has special covenants with the Jews and he has always protected and preserved his people. However, the Gentiles were excluded from this special relationship with God. While some Gentiles in the Old Testament came to believe in God (Ruth, for example), most had no knowledge or understanding of the one true God. Until Jesus.

Jesus is the Savior for all people, not only the Jews. Simeon understood that and he declared it when Jesus was just a baby, forty days old. Through the Holy Spirit, Simeon understood that it was God's plan to offer salvation to all people through Jesus.

I enjoy that Luke tells us that Mary and Joseph 'marveled' at what Simeon said about their boy. It's not like this was brand-new information. Instead, I think it never ceased to amaze them every time God sent assurances of his plan. Aren't we that way? We're surprised every time God gives us a wink. When we read the Bible and a verse stops us dead in our tracks because it speaks *exactly* to the very thing we're wrestling with. Or a sermon or a song or a sunset. There's no end to the ways that God shows us he's with us and that his words are unfailing.

Then, Simeon's words took a darker turn. I imagine him looking deep into Mary's eyes as he said quietly, "This child is destined to cause the falling and rising of many in Israel, and to be a sign that will be spoken against, so that the thoughts of many hearts will be revealed. And a sword will pierce your own soul too." (2:34-35) Simeon knew that the road ahead was not going to be easy. Although the Israelites

"In the birth stories of Matthew and Luke, only one person seems to grasp the mysterious nature of what God has set in motion: the old man Simeon, who recognized the baby as Messiah, instinctively understood that conflict would surely follow....Somehow Simeon sensed that though on the surface little had changed–the autocrat Herod still ruled, Roman troops were still stringing up patriots, Jerusalem still overflowed with beggars–underneath, everything had changed. A new force had arrived to undermine the world's powers."--Philip Yancey

had been waiting for the Anointed One, they would not embrace him. Perhaps Providentially just as Simeon was getting dark, Anna joined them. Of her, Luke wrote: "There was also a prophet, Anna, the daughter of Penuel, of the tribe of Asher. She was very old; she had lived with her husband seven years after her marriage, and then was a widow until she was eighty-four. She never left the temple but worshiped night and day, fasting and praying." (2:36-37)

This is an oddly specific lineage, especially for someone who only gets three verses total scene time. So, I looked into it for us and I discovered this is another one of those amazing little sequences only God could ordain.

- Anna, sometimes translated as Hannah harkens back to the Hannah of 2 Samuel. We talked about her briefly on The Magnificat Trail. Hannah in the Old Testament dedicated her son Samuel in the temple where he was blessed by the priest Eli. This Anna met Jesus on the day he was presented at the temple and blessed him.

- She was the daughter of Penuel. This first name is not mentioned anywhere else in the Bible, but we do find it in Genesis as a place name. It is the place where Jacob wrestled with God. He refused to let go until he was blessed, and God said, "Your name will no longer be Jacob, but Israel, because you have struggled with God and with humans and have overcome." The name 'Israel' likely means 'struggles with God'. In turn, Jacob named the place 'Penuel' which means 'face of God' as 'because I saw God face to face, and yet my life was spared.' (Genesis 32:28, 30). Here in Luke 2, Anna the daughter of Penuel, looks into the face of God and the salvation of Israel.

- She was of the tribe of Asher. There were twelve tribes of Israel. When the kingdom split, there were ten tribes in the northern kingdom of Israel and two in the southern kingdom of Judah. Asher was one of the ten tribes in the north. Eventually, they became one of the 'lost tribes' due to repeated conquest. Yet, here we see how God is bringing back what was lost. The scattered tribes of Israel are coming, however slowly, under the lordship of Christ the King.

Don't you just love the details? Over and over again we have seen that no detail is random. A simple sentence like 'Anna, daughter of Penuel of the tribe of Asher' is loaded with symbolism.

As a note here: The Bible tells us in Revelation 21:8 that John (who wrote the book of Revelation) "saw the holy city, new Jerusalem, coming down out of heaven from God". It is absolutely God's plan to redeem Jerusalem and his chosen people, the Jews. Someday when Jesus returns, this will happen. Jesus will redeem Jerusalem by creating a new one--a perfect one, one that will never be conquered by an enemy and will always exist in peace and freedom.

And there's more. In Deuteronomy 17 and 19, God instructed the Israelites that two or three witnesses were needed for a legal charge. Here at the temple, Simeon and Anna act as witnesses. Both confess Jesus as the Christ. Together they represent the human race, male and female. Pastor Dave Shaw writes: "The man comes first, but it is not good for him to be alone, so the woman comes second, joins to the work of the man, and together they complete their service to the Lord."

Simeon and Anna both waited all their lives to see the Savior. Perhaps their faithfulness in being willing to wait their entire lives showed God that they were the right people to deliver his message. And their words were not just for Mary and Joseph--they were for us as well. Because of Simeon and Anna, we know that God keeps his promises, he has a redemption plan, and it is for all people.

Dear Lord Jesus, there is so much to learn in the details of your life story. The faithfulness of your earthly parents reminds me to follow your commands. The faithfulness of Simeon and Anna reminds me to wait expectantly for your return. Thank you for the examples you have given me to emulate in your Word. Amen.

- Why do you think God told the Israelites to consecrate their **first born** sons to him?
- Think about a time when God spoke to you and you 'marveled'. How did he speak to you?
- Who did you tell? Remember, God tells us to be witnesses. In Christian circles, we often talk of 'sharing your testimony'. All that means is telling someone else what God has done as Anna did.

21) Waiting[9]

But about that day or hour no one knows, not even the angels in heaven, nor the Son, but only the Father. Be on guard! Be alert! You do not know when that time will come. –Mark 13:32-33

'O come, o come, Emmanuel, and ransom captive Israel who mourns in lonely exile here until the Son of God appear.'

We've been waiting for such a long time. Captive. In need of ransom. Exiled. Longing for home. Do you feel it? Deep inside–do you feel that longing? We've been waiting so long that sometimes we forget we're waiting. This is our normal, after all. It's all we've known. This waiting.

We've been waiting for such a long time.

We are the ancient Israelites waiting for the promised Messiah. Four hundred years of silence. Praying and waiting, waiting and praying. No prophets, only priests with the law rigidly kept and never enough. No pillar of cloud by day and pillar of fire by night. Those were the old days. The good days. These are the waiting days. Captivity, exile, mourning. See the gloomy clouds of night, feel death's dark shadows. It's hard to hold onto the promise of light after centuries of waiting.

We've been waiting for such a long time.

---

[9] I wrote this monologue to be read at my church in December 2022. The pastoral staff did a sermon series using Christmas Carols, and this monologue went with 'O Come, O Come, Emmanuel.' I decided to reuse it here as Simeon and Anna's story is so much about waiting well.

We are the Church, waiting for the return of the king. More than two thousand years have passed since God broke his silence with angels and miraculous babies–John to prepare the way for God's son and Jesus who would be the Way. We're waiting for the triumphant return Jesus promised. This time a warrior to end our battle with Darkness and make all things new. We have the joy of our salvation, secure in Christ's nail-pierced hands. And yet sometimes, if we're honest, the waiting is weary. Like Israelites of old, we long for home, exiles here in a weary, fallen world. Jesus, we are waiting.

We've been waiting for such a long time.

Yes, it is our normal. This waiting for Jesus is all we've known. It was normal for the Israelites too. Waiting was all they had known. Let's consider the legacy they left us: did they wait in watchful expectation? Or did their weariness overtake their wakefulness? It can be hard to remember that what we're waiting for is real and true and good in a world that is hell-bent on coaxing us to forget. Were they ready to receive the Savior when he came? Or did they miss Him, expecting someone else? It can be hard to live in the reality of who Jesus is and what he has done for us when the world whispers that we really need something else to feel good.

'Rejoice, rejoice, Emmanuel, has come to thee o Israel.' God is with us, Church. And we can wait with joyful, hopeful hearts for an eternity with Jesus, the Light of the World. What better time than Christmas to lean into waiting well?

It might be hard. With the kaleidoscope of festive distractions and our fast-paced lives, it can be difficult for our hearts to prepare him room. We become preoccupied with many things. But we can choose the better thing, the one thing that's needed. Worship. A deliberate time of anticipation. A time to invite Jesus into our lives all over again and break through the darkness of winter gloom and waiting. A time to celebrate our freedom in Christ. A time to rejoice because he has come and will come again.

We've been waiting for such a long time. May we wait well with watchful hearts and wakeful minds.

Jesus, enable us to wait well. Strengthen us. Comfort us. Turn our hearts to you. Don't let us get complacent or let our faith go cold. Wake us up when we get weary of waiting. Remind us of the future you promised. Jesus, you are our hope and our future. We are waiting. Amen.

- How has your Christmas season been unfolding? Where have distractions and busyness crowded in? Where have you been able to save space to contemplate the coming of Jesus?
- Think about Jesus's promised return. How do you feel about that? Do you think you're waiting well? What do you think it means to wait well?
- Jesus warned, "Because of the increase of wickedness, the love of most will grow cold, but the one who stands firm to the end will be saved." (Matt 24:12-13) As we wait for Jesus to return, it is so important that we don't let our love grow cold. How can you stand firm to the end?
- Consider the example of Simeon and Anna, and reflect on how you can imitate them as you wait for Jesus to return.

22) A Magi's Story

When they saw the star, they were overjoyed.-- Matthew 2:10

The Night sky has long been my pursuit of study. Of all the things I have learned and studied– mathematics, alchemy, medicine, history, interpretation of dreams–astronomy has been my greatest passion. There is beauty in the heavens: the stars in the firmament, the steady phases of the moon. Some of the other Magi preferred the other disciplines, but the stars have always spoken to me. Sometimes in ways I did not quite understand.

I was the first to notice the new star rising in the East. New stars are no ordinary thing. And this was no ordinary star. Indeed, I've never been quite sure it was a star exactly. However, I didn't know what else to call it–this great light. I tracked this star each night. I mapped its place in the sky and studied its path. After some brief discussion with the other Magi, I was certain it could only mean one thing: a new king had been born. An extraordinary king. The gods don't put new stars in the heavens for ordinary rulers and babies.

We consulted, studied, and talked for many days. I could think of nothing else but this great light. A most curious stirring filled my heart. I longed to see the One for whom it shone. I needed to find this infant king. I was compelled to worship him.

We decided to set out on a journey to follow this star. Gifts were needed to offer this newborn king. Gold and frankincense were chosen by my comrades; I chose myrrh. Myrrh is necessary for anointing kings, and as this was no ordinary king, I felt it was a great honor to offer the myrrh for his anointing.

The journey took us far from home. Following the star, the great light burned steady and true. Each day, though I was tired and weary at times, I felt the source of this light calling to me. *Come and worship the newborn king.* I have worshiped many gods and kings, and never felt a call such as this. I started to wonder: had I ever truly worshiped before? Or was it fear that moved me? Did I fear the gods and rulers, and only then regard them with any awe? This was different–I felt no fear when I gazed upon that star and thought about the One for whom it shone.

At last, we stopped in Jerusalem. We were certain, absolutely certain, that this star signified a newborn king of the Jews. And where else would we find a king of the Jews but in Jerusalem? But when we approached King Herod and his court, they were quite disturbed by our words. I saw fear in Herod's eyes. Fear, jealousy, suspicion. I have studied the stars, but I have also studied men and kings. I know when the king before me is of a dangerous kind, and this one was treacherous.

King Herod consulted his own Magi, though that's not what the Jews call them–**chief priests and teachers of the law.** They in turn consulted their scriptures and prophets. They came to one conclusion: Bethlehem. Herod called us in–secretly–and asked us when we first noted the star. I was loath to tell this man, yet I was in no position to lie to him either. He congratulated us on our wisdom and knowledge, on our proficiency in astronomy and navigation–flattering words that didn't stir my heart. Then, he sent us on our way, saying: **"Go and search carefully for the child. As soon as you find him, report to me, so that I too may go and worship him."**

We turned towards Bethlehem, a tiny little town only a few hours' journey from Jerusalem. Sure enough, it was over this town that the star came to rest. Never before had I seen a star move as this one did. Never before had I seen a star settle so obviously over one town. More than that, never before had I seen a star settle above a single home.

A tiny little home in this tiny little town. A house with a carpenter's workshop, and a peasant's wife in the kitchen. How was this possible?

At once I felt two things: I was baffled that this humble place could be the home of a great king, and I was overjoyed that I would soon behold the king. That stirring I had felt for so long now swelled with rapture I'd never felt before or since. Trembling, I took my gift of myrrh and blinked away tears from my tired eyes. What kind of king could make me feel like this?

"We've come to worship the newborn king," I explained to the child's mother. He was hiding behind her leg, a chubby wobbly little mite with brown eyes that shone like stars. In her eyes, I read wonder...but no fear. She did not fear me or my fellow Magi, even though she must have thought we were dressed strangely and spoke strangely. Jews are a most peculiar and fastidious type–they have strict rules about Gentiles. It was entirely possible that we would've come all this way and be shut out because we were unclean, according to their tradition. Unclean and unwelcome. I hoped our prestige as Magi would earn her favor.

The mother gave us a long, thoughtful look, and then opened the door for us to come in. Quietly, we entered their small home and the child climbed into his mother's lap. He didn't appear to be extraordinary, only a little peasant child. He smiled at us and babbled as wee ones do saying words only really understood by his mother. We worshiped him anyway. Bowing

114

low before him, I knew in my heart that I had never truly worshiped before. I was driven by something greater than ritual or fear; I was drawn by his presence. Somehow I felt that looking into his tender face, I was looking at the face of God. Here, in this tiny house in a tiny town unfit for a king.

We offered the child our gifts which his mother received most gratefully. I couldn't help but wonder how gifts like ours would change their lives: gold, frankincense, and myrrh must be riches beyond their wildest dreams. The mother looked at each one with a depth of wonder I have rarely seen outside of my sect of Magi.

"Thank you," I said as we prepared to leave their home and set up camp outside the village for the night. "I cannot quite understand it, but I know your child will be a very great king. Why else would the gods honor him with a star?"

"He is the Son of the Most High," she smiled. Her eyes looked up to the heavens, just as mine have done every night for as long as I can remember. "The Son of God. Emmanuel–God with us."

God with us. Was I really in the presence of God? I looked down once more on the child and he grinned up at me, holding onto his mother's finger. I couldn't explain it–but I knew it was true.

We slept under the stars that night, basking in the glow of that great light that had led us on this journey. A dream came to us, each and every one. Only the Most High could give us all such a dream. In it was a warning to not return to King Herod, but to go home another way. We were unanimously agreed to do as we were warned. King Herod was not a man to be trusted, nor a man to trifle with. We traveled home as far away from Jerusalem as we could get.

Later, we heard the news of King Herod's atrocity in Bethlehem. When he realized we had outwitted him, **he was furious, and he gave orders to kill all the boys in Bethlehem and its vicinity who were two years old and under, in accordance with the time he had learned from** us. Oh, the mourning that must have filled that tiny town. We wondered if the family escaped–surely the Son of the Most High would be spared. God himself would make a way. He must have.

I've often studied the stars for a sign to tell me if the child lives. But the great light doesn't shine anymore. Yet, in the darkest part of the night, when I think back on that day I feel as though the great light shines inside me. That the child *is* the light, and darkness cannot overcome it. Yes, I am certain He lives. And because of him, the world is changed. I am changed.

- What is your attitude in worship? Like the Magi in my account prior to the star, do you 'worship' going through the motions? Or are you like the Magi after the star and excited about coming to worship? Do you worship with joy? Wonder?
- What makes worship hard? Distractions? Difficulties? Routine?

23) A True Story

After Jesus was born in Bethlehem in Judea, during the time of
King Herod, Magi from the east came to Jerusalem and asked,
"Where is the one who has been born king of the Jews? We saw his star when
it rose and have come to worship him."-- Matthew 2:1-2

★**Read Matthew 2:1-23**

It occurred to me that the people and plot twists in the visit of the Magi
read like a great fairy tale. Theologian C.S. Lewis was a lover of fairy tales,
and a scholar and expert in them
as well. He didn't shy away from
the 'mythical' elements of the
Christ story. Instead, he called it
'the one true myth'. I understand
if this probably makes at least
some of you uncomfortable. But
I truly don't think God is
offended. He is the original
storyteller, and all our stories are
but echoes and poor reflections
of the epic narrative of his story

> "Now the story of Christ is simply a
> true myth: a myth working on us the
> same way as the others, but with this
> tremendous difference that it really
> happened: and one must be content to
> accept it in the same way, remembering
> that it is God's myth where the others
> are men's myths: i.e., the Pagan stories
> are God expressing Himself through
> the minds of poets, using such images
> as He found there, while Christianity is
> God expressing Himself through what
> we call 'real things'."-- C.S. Lewis

of redeeming his beloved. Here in Matthew 2, we find a monstrous villain,
wise men on a journey, stars and angels and dreams, and a young family on
the run for their lives. Let's take a closer look, starting with the villain and
the wise men, shall we?

It's been mentioned before that the Jews were actually under Roman rule.
So, you might be wondering, why do they have a king? The Romans

allowed the Jews to have their own king but he had to report to the Emperor in Rome. He could rule over the Jewish people, but not anyone else living in Israel. King Herod was approved by Rome because he would do whatever he was told. In fact, Herod was only half-Jewish even though he was king of the Jews. The Jews didn't trust him or like him because he did many, many evil things during his reign.

Herod the Great is famous for two main things: being a prolific builder, and being a paranoid, ruthless despot. Under his leadership, many building projects were completed including rebuilding of the temple in Jerusalem. However, he also had many people put to death including members of the Jewish Sanhedrin, his wife, and several of his own sons. He feared that when he died the people would not mourn him, so he ordered that many of his highest ranking officials would be executed after his death. As it turns out, after Herod the Great died no one saw the sense in following this deranged order and their lives were spared.

The Magi were very well-educated men who studied ancient prophecies, the stars, and many other things for wisdom. They're often called "the three kings" but that's just tradition based on the three gifts named in the scripture. The Bible does not say that there were three of them or that they were kings. They did happen to be very learned and 'wise men', so *that* nickname fits. They came from 'the East', probably Babylon or Persia.

Now that we have that settled, let's return to the text. Right away we find out that Herod was disturbed by their inquiry. He wasn't the rightful king of the Jews and he knew it. Also, remember that the Jews were expecting someone who would free them from the Romans. Herod might have worried that the Messiah would overthrow him as king and rule over Israel instead. Plus, this man was already riddled with paranoia. It didn't take much to disturb him.

Interestingly, Herod seemed aware that prophecies existed concerning a Messiah, or perhaps the rightful heir to David's throne, but he was clearly not well-versed. Unlike King David in the glory days of Israel's past, King Herod's heart was far from God and his mind was not concerned with the things of God. Concerned only for his own power, Herod became an enemy of God.

Matthew wrote that all of Jerusalem was troubled because Herod was troubled. The court officials, chief priests, and scribes likely feared for their own lives because Herod was so unstable and violent. The chief priests and scribes reported to him Micah's prophecy: 'But you, Bethlehem, in the land of Judah, are by no means least among the rulers of Judah; for out of you will come a ruler who will shepherd my people Israel.' (Mic 5:2). Let us notice that none of these Jewish scholars or priests went to find the baby for themselves. Maybe they thought the Magi were quacks, or maybe they were afraid of King Herod, but none were curious enough to investigate for themselves.

Before the Magi went on their way, Herod asked them when exactly the star appeared and he directed them to return so he could also worship the child. I can almost see him twisting his Snidely Whiplash mustache.

In Ancient times, stars had significant meaning. The Magi studied them carefully and made note of all the movements of the stars and planets in the night sky. Whenever they saw something out of the ordinary, they believed it was a sign or a message. In this case, they believed it was a sign of a new divine king.

Much has been written about the star. It likely was not a literal star, as stars don't appear and move and disappear like this one. Many astronomers believe it was a conjunction of the planets. Messianic Rabbi Jason Sobel

119

asserts it wasn't a star but 'a great light', meaning a supernatural event. In his book *Mysteries of the Messiah,* he explains other incidents in scripture of 'a great light' and what it symbolized and foretold. I am no scientist or scholar, so it's not for me to say what the star was or was not. Ultimately, I don't believe it matters (although it's interesting to research and think about). What matters is that a group of learned Gentile pagans observed an anomaly in the night sky, interpreted that it meant the birth of a new and significant king, and went to find him.

What's more, this great light led them to the very place. The shepherds were given a unique sign: a baby wrapped in swaddling cloths and lying in a manger. The Magi could only follow the light. There's no indication that they knocked on every door in town. Instead, scripture reports that the star 'stopped over the place where the child was' (Matt 2:10).

In verse eleven, we read that the Magi came to 'the house'. We know that Jesus was born in a stable because there was no room for Mary and Joseph anywhere else in Bethlehem. Bible scholars have debated what the stable was like, whether or not there was really an inn, or if it was a house. And they've also debated where the Magi arrived to worship Jesus. The bottom line is: we don't know *for sure* if they were in Bethlehem or possibly Nazareth. I believe they were in Bethlehem based on the textual evidence in Matthew. But we do know, the wise men were not in the manger with the shepherds. They were not there the night Jesus was born.

The star *appeared* the night Jesus was born. The Magi had to research it, follow it, talk to Herod, follow it some more, and then find Jesus. Jesus could have possibly been two years old by this time--although, most scholars think he was around a year old.

But setting all those details aside, let's focus on what the Magi came to do--worship Jesus! When they found him, the Magi were overjoyed. Imagine this band of foreign men, important and prestigious in their own land quivering with joy like puppies. As I write, I find myself longing for a measure of their joy.

They worshiped him and brought him very expensive, precious gifts. This must've been another incredulous moment for Mary and Joseph. They were ordinary, and likely, poor people. Joseph was a carpenter and Mary was just an ordinary young woman. Matthew doesn't report that Joseph was home during the Magi's visit. Imagine Mary at home while Joseph is working. Perhaps she was baking bread, or maybe Jesus was fussing. After all, he was a baby heading into toddlerhood, and those little ones sure can fuss. And then these wise men from another country show up to worship Jesus and to give them extraordinarily valuable gifts. This had to have been even more shocking than the shepherds arriving the night he was born, and Simeon's words at the temple. I grin as I picture Mary explaining it all to him, showing him the treasures they gave their son. If Mary and Joseph were anything at all like most of the married couples I know, she had to explain it all over two or three times. And I imagine her laughing, maybe with tears in her eyes from both joy and wonder at God's provision.

Because God surely was providing. It turns out that Jesus's parents needed that gift of gold far more than the Magi could've imagined when they set out to find this newborn king. Remember that all this worship and joy is threatened by the despot King Herod. The Magi were warned in a dream to not return to him, and Joseph was warned to get the heck out of Dodge. Er, Bethlehem. In fact, he was told to take his fledgling family to Egypt.

This was not the first time a man named Joseph ended up in Egypt and God used him to protect and preserve his people (the seed of Abraham through whom all people would be blessed). All the way back in Genesis 37-50, there was a young man named Joseph who had prophetic dreams. The life of this Joseph was full of hardships, yet God sustained him. I wish I had the space to outline how the Old Testament Joseph acts as a predecessor to Jesus, and the additional similarities between OT Joe and NT Joe. I don't because it's *a lot*. It suffices to repeat: nothing here is random. If you've ever wondered why New Testament Joseph had all those dreams, I believe it's because Old Testament Joseph also was a dreamer and our God loves symmetry and symbolism.

Joseph led Mary and Jesus on a return journey to Egypt. The very place Moses (and his sister Miriam–remember her when we talked about Mary's name as a variant of Miriam?) escaped in the Exodus. I wonder what thoughts may have swirled in their minds as they became refugees. Did the history and promises of the Exodus provide comfort? Did it ease their fears to know that God had delivered their people from this land before, and surely he would make a way for them to come home someday?

And God did bring them home. Matthew does not specify how long they were in Egypt. History tells us Herod the Great died in 4 BC. Jesus was likely born between 7 BC and 4 BC (a monk named Dionysius is responsible for the calculating error that distorts the BC/AD record of Jesus's birth by a few years).

It's safe to assume they weren't in Egypt for many years, though their return home may not have happened directly after Herod the Great died. We read that when Joseph realized Archelaus was the new king, he was afraid to go back to Judea. Herod Archelaus was the principal heir to

Herod the Great. He reigned for ten years and became so unpopular with the Jews that Rome deposed him as king and exiled him to Gaul. I think Joseph had good reason to fear this man.

We talked at length before about Joseph's persevering faith in God during hardships and life plot twists. I want to pause for a moment to talk specifically about fear. About ten years ago I wrote some women's Bible study lessons, one of which was on fear. And this was the text I used.

I am *sure* Joseph was afraid. Matthew told us he was afraid. It is not a sin to be afraid when things are scary. Life *is* scary sometimes. We live in a fallen world corrupted by evil. There are dangers. Being dismissive or cavalier about that doesn't get you brownie points. In fact, if we become prideful in the face of danger and mock fear then I think we've gotten off track. Fear should turn us toward God. When Joseph was afraid, he trusted and obeyed God. Remember what Gabriel said to Mary? 'The Lord is with you...No word from God will ever fail.' (Luke 1:28, 37). Perhaps Mary and Joseph repeated these words to one another time and again as they trusted God through every dark turn in the road. And we can surely trust these words too.

> To be clear, the Bible instructs us not to fear over 300 times. God does not want us to allow fear to control us, to limit us, or to weaken our faith. My assertion is that when we do experience fear it is meant to draw us toward God, greater dependence on him which is exercised in trusting and obeying.

If our fear paralyzes us and we don't move in the way God directs, we've fallen into sin. If we become reckless in the face of danger to show we are not afraid, we have also fallen into sin. Joseph could have returned to Judea to show that he wasn't going to let fear control him, but he would not have been obeying God. This would've been most unwise, and even tempting God as Jesus said we are not to do. When we are afraid, or confronted with danger or hardship, we should strive to be like Joseph. Here's an easy phrase to remember: When you are afraid, trust and obey.

Returning to the text, the danger of Archelaus was why Joseph was told to take his family back to Galilee. The holy family ended up in Nazareth, where Mary and Joseph's story began. Nazareth was out of the jurisdiction of Archelaus. More than that, prophecy foretold the savior would come from Galilee. And as we well know by now, no word from God ever fails.

Additionally, I believe this is how we can reconcile Matthew's record with Luke's account. Looking at Luke 2, we read that after the presentation at the temple Mary and Joseph returned home to Galilee. It was here that Jesus 'grew in wisdom and stature, and in favor with God and man.' (Luke 2:40). Luke's version leaves out the escape to Egypt. Perhaps this supports the idea that they weren't there for a prolonged amount of time. Either way, both Matthew and Luke agree Jesus was raised in Nazareth.

I wish we were given vignettes from his early childhood. I want to know about his first words and favorite foods. I wonder what his favorite stories were to hear. Maybe he liked to tell jokes and he talked Joseph's ear off when he spent time with him in his shop. If we needed to know, surely the Bible would tell us. As it is, I'm grateful this story of the Magi was included–a true story of light triumphing over darkness.

Father God, this is such a wondrous story. I am so thankful it's a true story. I love seeing your provision and protection so that nothing–not even a villainous king–could stop your plan. Amen

- Epiphany has been celebrated for over a thousand years. The Christmas carol "The Twelve Days of Christmas" is about The Epiphany, the twelve days *after* Christmas. Check out this QR code for an article from Christianity.com about the song's coded meaning.

- What do you do when you feel afraid? Do you lean in and trust God? Are you tempted to make your own plans and trust your own wisdom?

- Has there ever been a time when you allowed danger to make you prideful to show that you weren't afraid when others were?

- Think back over the Christmas narrative. Who came to worship Jesus? Who heard about him and didn't come to see for themselves? Why did some come to worship, and others didn't? Why do some come today and others don't?

24) We Have Seen His Glory

For to us a child is born, to us a son is given,
and the government will be on his shoulders.
And he will be called Wonderful Counselor, Mighty God,
Everlasting Father, Prince of Peace. –Isaiah 9:6

★ **Read Isaiah 9:1-7**

The opening lines of Isaiah 9 are some of my favorites. This should not surprise you given what I shared of my love for the Gospel of John and his use of dark and light. In his prophecy of the distant future, Isaiah declared: "Nevertheless, there will be no more gloom for those who were in distress... The people walking in darkness have seen a great light; on those living in the land of deep darkness a light has dawned." (1:1) The New Living Translation says: "Nevertheless, that time of darkness and despair will not go on forever." I stumbled across that verse in a season of struggling, when it seemed that nothing but trouble stretched out in front of me forever and ever. God's Word is a healing balm with promises we can lean into when we need them most.

Isaiah 9:6 is often repeated at Christmas. In the original material, I broke down each part of this verse for kids so they could get a complete picture of the promise. Allow me to share an abridged version with you:

- "...and the government will be on his shoulders.": Someday Jesus will be the leader of the entire world. And he will do it perfectly. He won't make mistakes. He won't make bad choices or selfish choices. His plans will be for the benefit of all people. He will be able to govern in perfect peace.

- "And he will be called Wonderful Counselor...": He is able to advise us through every situation we face. We can trust that his instruction and advice are perfect. Because Jesus is our Wonderful Counselor, we can go to him freely and be comforted. He not only tells us what to do, but he comforts us as well.

- "...Mighty God...": Jesus cannot be defeated. He cannot be stopped. No one can overcome his power. Whatever the problem is, Jesus is mighty enough to conquer it.

- "...Everlasting Father...": Wait a minute, everlasting *father*? Most people think this verse is a reference to the Trinity. However, it's actually a poor translation. The better translation is 'Father of Eternity' (Young's Literal Translation). Jesus is the only way to eternal life. Having a personal relationship with Jesus as your savior is the only way we get to spend the rest of eternity in heaven. Because Jesus made salvation possible and he's the only way to get there, Isaiah called him 'Father of Eternity'.

- "...Prince of Peace.": In Biblical times, a prince was not merely the son of a king. A prince was a ruler with power and authority. A good prince works to keep his people safe and well cared for. Jesus is the Prince of Peace. His kingdom is one of peace. The people he cares for--us--are given peace in his kingdom.

This short verse, so often repeated this time of year, packs a very powerful punch. The picture it paints of Jesus is nothing short of glorious. This feels like a good place for us to look back and remember all the things that have been said about Jesus.

Jesus Is...

- He is the Word made flesh who dwelled among us
- He is Emmanuel–God with us
- He is the Lamb of God who takes away the sins of the world
- He is the Good Shepherd who lays down his life and takes it up again
- He is the Anointed One, Messiah, Christ
- He is the Lord, supreme authority
- He is Yeshua, salvation, deliverer
- He is the Son of the Most High, Son of God
- He is the Root of Jesse, the Son of David
- He is the Seed of Abraham, Isaac, and Jacob through him all will be blessed
- He is the Seed of Eve who crushes the head of the serpent
- He is the consolation of Israel and the redemption of Jerusalem
- He is the light for the Gentiles
- He is a perfect leader
- He is a perfect counselor and comforter
- His might and power cannot be broken or defeated
- He makes salvation and eternal life possible
- He offers us peace in his kingdom

And in Isaiah 9:7 we read these beautiful words: "Of the greatness of his government and peace there will be no end."

All of this was wrapped up in swaddling cloths and placed in a manger. Now I feel something akin to what the Magi felt when their journey stopped and they found him!

Our journey is coming to a close here. Have you found him? Have you found your wonder again? I surely hope so. Let's look back at the verse we prayed in the second reading.

> The Word became flesh and made his dwelling among us. We have seen his glory, the glory of the one and only Son, who came from the Father, full of grace and truth.-- John 1:14

We've listened to Elizabeth, Mary, Joseph, Gabriel, Anna, a shepherd, and a Magi tell us how they beheld the glory of the Messiah. I pray we have seen it too, and that we haven't missed it as so many did two thousand years ago.

I want to close today with a bit of personal testimony. As I've written this book, God has been so faithful. I don't quite know how to describe the process. I started with an outline which I rewrote and rewrote before I finally realized: I couldn't map this out. I just had to show up and see what God wanted to say. In every chapter, God has revealed something to me, and I pray I've adequately shared it with you.

The other night I paused my writing to take my puppy for a walk. We live in a quiet neighborhood so I prayed aloud as we walked and Teddy sniffed things. I told God how grateful I was for this experience, especially since life has been fraught with difficulty at the same time. The deeper I got into writing, sometimes it seemed the harder life was getting (don't even get me started on the issues I ran into as this book got closer and closer to publication). How could I write about trusting God when I was struggling so much? How could I tell you about worship when I had so many worries?

Because it's never been about what I know. It's about *who* I know. It's always been about who God is and what he does. My friends, if you only take away one thing from this book please let it be this:

No word from God will ever fail. With God nothing is impossible.

On my walk that evening with my puppy, I realized this is what I've come to know deep in my bones. It's no longer just something I've read or heard or repeated. This has become part of me. I pray it becomes part of you too.

In the darkest nights of the soul, there's no greater hope than the one we have in Jesus. The Word made flesh. The King who is coming back. We can bet the farm on it because no word from God will ever fail and with him nothing is impossible. The circumstances in our lives–individually, nationally, globally–cannot thwart his plans.

'For the word of the Lord is right and true; he is faithful in all he does... the plans of the Lord stand firm forever, the purposes of his heart through all generations'. – Psalm 33:4, 11

Christmas is a time to celebrate the goodness of God's plans and his faithfulness. We can wrap his love tight around us and rest in it. And we can pass it on through all generations. There's no greater gift than Jesus.

Dear Lord Jesus, I am filled with wonder at the glory of you. Everything you are, everything you have done, and everything you are preparing even now. Help me to live in the reality that your word never fails and that nothing is impossible with you. Thank you that I can take comfort in this beautiful truth, even as I'm filled with wonder and awe. May your praises ever be on my lips as I tell others about you. Amen.

- Remember when I asked you to jot down what you wanted to feel this Christmas and then pray over that list? Use this space to reflect on how this Christmas season has unfolded. Has it been what you expected? Wanted? Needed? How have you seen and experienced Jesus at work? Where have you needed more of him? What praises can you offer him?

25) Epilogue

The story is warm and familiar, like a quilt passed through generations. The story of a king born long ago, a king who came to save the whole world. We tell it again and again and again so we never forget. Jesus, the son of God, born to save the world. A miracle of love we can hardly comprehend, and the joy of our salvation.

The story of the first birthday of the King.

You know the story, how the angels came to the shepherds while they were tending their sheep. How the shepherds ran to find the Christ child and then told everyone they met their glorious, good news.

You know about the star, shining in the east, and leading the Magi to the King of Kings. And when they found the Christ child, they worshiped him and gave him gifts. You know the gifts–gold, frankincense, and myrrh.

You know of God's great love for us. His perfect plan to rescue his people, to bring his people from exile and captivity. To bring us home.

Tell this story again and again, and tell it well. Tell it as we wait for the King to come again. Tell it to your children and your children's children. Tell it to your friends and neighbors. And when you grow weary and tired, tell it to yourself again. Hold it tight around you, but never lose your wonder.

'Today in the town of David, a Savior has been born to you; he is Christ the Lord! Glory to God in the highest, and on earth peace, goodwill to men.' (Luke 2:11)

Selected Bibliography

Ellicott, Charles. "Ellicott's Commentary for English Readers on Matthew 1." Bible Hub. 18 Mar, 2014. Web. <https://biblehub.com/commentaries/ellicott/matthew/1.htm>

Gallagher, Timothy M. *Meditation and Contemplation: An Ignatian Guide to Praying with Scripture.* Crossroad Publishing Company, 2008.

Guzik, David. "Study Guide for Luke 1." Blue Letter Bible. 6/2022. Web. <https://www.blueletterbible.org/comm/guzik_david/study-guide/luke/luke-1.cfm>.

Grondin, Fr. Charles. "Long-Lived Apostles? Not so Much." Catholic Answers, Catholic Answers, 23 Feb. 2019, <www.catholic.com/qa/long-lived-apostles-not-so-much.>

Henry, Matthew. "Commentary on Luke 1." Blue Letter Bible. 1 Mar, 1996. Web. <https://www.blueletterbible.org/Comm/mhc/Luk/Luk_001.cfm>. –"Commentary on Luke 2." Blue Letter Bible. 1 Mar, 1996. Web. <https://www.blueletterbible.org/Comm/mhc/Luk/Luk_002.cfm>.

Lewis, Clive Staples. "To Arthur Greeves." 1 Oct 1931. *CS Lews Collected Letters.* HarperOne, 2009.

Smith, Chuck. "Verse by Verse Study on Luke 1 (C2000)." Blue Letter Bible. 1 Jun, 2005. Web. <https://www.blueletterbible.org/Comm/smith_chuck/c2000_Luk/Luk_001.cfm>.

Sobel, Rabbi Jason. Mysteries of the Messiah. Thomas Nelson, 2021.

Spurgeon, Charles. "The First Christmas Carol." Blue Letter Bible. 18 Apr, 2001. Web. <https://www.blueletterbible.org/Comm/spurgeon_charles/sermons/0168.cfm>.

Yancey, Philip. "Chapter 2: Birth: The Visited Planet." The Jesus I Never Knew, Zondervan Pub. House, Grand Rapids, MI, 1995.

Recommended Reading

Although these books are not quoted directly in *Possible*, I cannot recommend them enough.

Johnston, Jeremiah J, PHD. *Body of Proof: The 7 Best Reasons to Believe in the Resurrection of Jesus–and Why it Matters Today.* Bethany House Publishers. Minneapolis, Minnesota, 2023.

Eldredge, John. *Beautiful Outlaw: Experiencing the Playful, Disruptive, Extravagant Personality of Jesus.* Faith Words. Hachette Book Group. New York, NY, 2011.

Acknowledgements

No book comes into the world without help–including this one. First and foremost, thanks go to Amy Schulz, my mother. She read through various incarnations of this material from 2020 to 2023, giving feedback, correcting punctuation, and encouraging me to keep going. Being able to partner with her on projects like this is such a gift.

Although I'm sure he's not expecting it my pastor, Mike O'Bryant, deserves thanks here. Last year just when I thought I was done writing things like this, he asked me to write some monologues for Christmastime. He told me what he was thinking then added, "You can really do whatever you want though." He left a creative door open and God showed up spectacularly in that space. Because of that opportunity, God was able to show me he still has words for me to share–words to glorify him and words to encourage weary hearts. And this summer, Pastor Mike encouraged me to write a Christmas book. I'm not sure this is what he had in mind–but then again, it's not really what I had in mind either. God showed up in this space, just like he did before.

And I have to thank my husband and my kids. They listen to my ideas, let me chatter about tidbits of discovery in my research, and give me opinions on things like titles, cover design, and fonts. It's not always easy when I'm hunkered down with earbuds in and my laptop on–ignoring laundry and dishes and other household chores. But they don't complain. When I'm discouraged, they tell me to keep going. And they remind me to take breaks for episodes of *Full House* or cups of hot cocoa on the front porch. Balance, you know?

About the Author

Insatiable curiosity, a background in literature, and a decent internet connection are what I bring to the table; God does all the rest. My husband Curtis and I have been married for 15 years, we have two awesome kids, and a Lassie-in-Training. If I'm not writing or with the kids, you can usually find me with my nose in a book.

Follow me on social media under the handle Plotting Possibility to stay in the know on future projects. For more of my books, check out: www. amazon.com/author/rebeccaberry

Scan this QR code for a link to my Amazon Author Page:

Made in the USA
Monee, IL
02 November 2023

45655528R00083